Education
Tax
Credit
Essentials

Dana Bell, EA

Thank you for purchasing this book. You are welcome to share this **Essentials edition** with your colleagues. This edition may be reproduced, copied and distributed, provided the book remains in its complete original form and no fee is charged. Send book feedback to edcredit@tylerhosting.com.

If you find this text useful and did not purchase it, please consider supporting the author by purchasing your own copy. This book is also available in several digital formats.

ISBN: 978-1-329-17742-0

All product or company names that may be mentioned in this publication are tradenames, trademarks or registered trademarks of their respective owners.

Table of Contents

Preface

In 2014 the Department of Treasury released a 4-page document explaining in part, how taxpayers can coordinate their Pell grant with qualifying expenses to maximize their education credit. That document also has a section that explains how to help with the appeal to "inform students that they have a choice in how to allocate Pell Grants for tax purposes."

Not only do students need to be aware of the potential of Pell grants and educational expenses, so do their parents, educational institutions, financial planners, and tax professionals. While I am not responding to that particular appeal, I am using this text to try to encourage others, with a focus on tax professionals, to learn more about education tax credits.

This text started as a series of articles on the blog Switched Keys describing how to claim education credits. The articles and other resources are also part of an AOTC toolkit that can be downloaded from www.tylerhosting.com/EdCredit/. Watch for the expanded version of this text, including updates and additional resources. Comments, questions, and corrections are welcome and can be submitted through the contact form on the blog, or directly to edcredit@tylerhosting.com. I have discovered a couple of issues during the writing and publishing process and I am sure I have omitted information that you might think useful and relevant. Let me know.

Meeting the Challenge

The tax code and regulations concerning education tax credits are relatively straightforward. In practice, however, education credits present a number of challenges. The first challenge in characterizing scholarships and grants is determining which scholarships are unrestricted, or elective. That requires understanding the differences between scholarships and doing some research. The second challenge is determining qualifying expenses as the document that contains that information may not be complete or accurate. The final challenge is educating clients about education credits. Educating clients may be the first step in the preparation, but professionals need to have a firm grip on education credits and the many ramifications of financing education.

Education credits were first introduced in 1998 but they have been expanded or extended three times. They are now good until 2017 but they will likely be extended or expanded again before that expiration.

The theory of education credits is really simple. Taxpayers can earn a credit for amounts paid for qualifying expenses. Even when you consider that those amounts are reduced by the amount of scholarships, it's an easy concept. The complexities come in when you have to determine qualified expenses, when you can include some scholarships in income, when you must research the nature of scholarships, and when you coordinate with other benefits and other aspects of the tax return. The goal of this text is to help you plan the process of calculating education credits.

Following are the basics you need to know to prepare returns with education credits

- Understanding the Education Credits
- Understanding the Regulations
- Researching Scholarships
- Document Preparation
- Student Account Tabulation
- Tax Credit Calculation

Additionally there are some suggestions for more efficient processes, effective strategies, and tax planning

- Tax Preparation Techniques
- Software Solutions
- Special Issues
- Documentation
- Planning and Coordination
- Amending for Education Credits

There are only two education credits under the current tax code and this book focuses primarily on the American Opportunity Tax Credit. Brief discussions of the Lifetime Learning Credit and various deductions are also included.

In The Beginning

In the beginning Congress created deductions for educational expenses but taxpayers could only enjoy those deductions if certain rules were followed. Deductions were decreases in taxable income. If there was no taxable income, there was no benefit. At that time scholarships were considered tax-free if used for qualified expenses.

Then there were credits. In 1998 the Hope Scholarship Credit was established that allowed taxpayers to claim expenses that were paid for qualified educational expenses during the first two years of college. These credits reduced the actual tax that was due, rather than lower taxable income as deductions. Of course, if the taxpayer did not owe any tax then he could not reduce that tax. The related Lifetime Learning Credit was also available but none of it was refundable either.

Over the years changes were made to the available credits. In 2009 the American Recovery and Reinvestment Act enhanced the Hope Credit, giving it a new name, the American Opportunity Tax Credit. It also made a portion of it refundable allowing taxpayers to consider the credit as a payment, which could be refunded even if he did not owe any tax. In 2011, the credit was extended through 2012 by the Tax Relief and Job Creation Act of 2010. In 2012 the AOTC was extended through 2017 by the American Taxpayer Relief Act of 2012.

Overview

The American Opportunity Tax Credit (AOTC or AOC) allows taxpayers to get a credit for $4,000 of qualified educational expenses. The total credit could amount to $2,500 in tax reduction. The first $2,000 is a 100% credit and the second $2,000 is a 25% credit. Only 40% of the AOTC is refundable so the maximum refund without tax reduction is $1,000. The Lifetime Learning Credit (LLC) is a 20% credit for up to $10,000 of educational expenses to gain or improve job skills. None of the LLC is refundable.

Taxpayers must choose between the LLC and the AOTC however, as they cannot claim both credits for the same student. If either credit is used, the tuition deduction is not allowed for that student. You can, however, claim the AOTC for one student and the LLC for another. There are also phase-outs for both credits. Lower income taxpayers are likely to use the American Opportunity Credit since it does not require taxable income for the refundable part of the credit. Some of the rules for AOTC are that the student must have been at least half-time and seeking a recognized educational credential.

When you search the web for education credits, this is often all that you will find on many websites. In many cases, the website is so out of date that it may mention the Hope Credit instead of the American Opportunity Tax Credit, and refer to the first two years instead of the first four years of undergraduate study. Still, there are other aspects of the credits that are not well known. For example, the regulations allow students to include some of their scholarships in income to increase the credit. Very often that is not mentioned.

The Regulations section later discusses that treatment along with other ways to coordinate the many other education benefits that may be used. There is a maze of other educational benefits that are available which may be more advantageous depending on the taxpayer's income level, tax bracket and other circumstances. For example, if you are in the 25% marginal tax bracket then the AOTC or a deduction would probably be more advantageous than the 20% LLC. Many other circumstances could affect your decision as well.

Note: It has been said that the American Opportunity Tax Credit replaces the Hope Credit. That is only partially true. The rules for AOTC modify the requirements for the Hope Credit and are good through tax year 2017, but the Hope Credit is not limited in time. Unless Congress makes changes in the law the Hope Credit will still be good in 2018 and later.

What You Need to Know

What you need to know about education credits depends on who you are. The IRS categorizes knowledge requirements for schools, 1098T filers, and tax preparers. If the taxpayer is preparing their own return they would be the tax preparer. The IRS webpage provides a summary of those "need to know" facts at http://www.eitc.irs.gov/Other-Refundable-Credits/aotcllc.

This text is primarily focused on what the tax preparer needs to know about the education credits to prepare returns and provide advice to clients. However, the client needs to know enough about education credits to see the benefits of providing the preparer the necessary information. The primary "need to know" facts include qualifications, qualifying expenses, and qualifying payments. The sections following discuss those elements for each of the credits.

Preparers will also need to gather relevant taxpayer information from client-provided documents or through the interview process. Additionally, an understanding of 1098T information and limitations is crucial to preparing accurate returns.

American Opportunity Tax Credit

Qualifications

Separate qualifications for the AOTC relate to the taxpayer and the student. The taxpayer (often a parent) must be claiming a dependency exemption for the student in order to claim the AOTC. Students qualifying for the AOTC can be any dependent for which you are allowed to take a dependency exemption (IRC § 25A(f)(1)(A)(iii)), including individuals that meet the test for dependency exemption as a qualifying relative. So, it's possible to claim the credit for a student who is a parent or a person whom you support and who lives with you all year (IRC § 152).

If the taxpayer is the student, he must be claiming his own exemption, and not be claimed by someone else. One of the pitfalls of the taxpayer qualifications is that a married student must file a joint return in order for the taxpayer to claim the credit (Treas. Reg. § 1.25A-1(g)).

Generally, once that is done the rest of the qualifications relate to the student. If the student meets the qualifications then the taxpayer qualifies to claim the credit. Some of the qualifications for the AOTC include.

- Student must be pursuing an undergraduate degree or other recognized education credential
- Student must be enrolled at least half time for at least one academic period beginning during the year
- No felony drug conviction on student's record
- Available for first 4 years of post secondary education
- Cannot be claimed more than 4 tax years.

Again, the credit is attached to the dependency exemption, so if a parent claims the AOTC for a child, the child will not be able to claim it. However, all expenses related to the child are claimed on that credit, whether paid by the student, or parent, or a third party (if paid to the institution). Additional qualifications for the taxpayer include an income threshold and phase-out. Currently the credit is available for taxpayers with a MAGI of less than $90,000 ($180,000 joint returns). MAGI takes into consideration several foreign deductions and exclusions.

Refundable Qualifications

Additional qualifications exist for the refundable portion of the credit. Students age 24 and over qualify for the refundable portion of the credit, as well as parents of children under the age of 24 if they claim the child as a dependent. While many students under the age of 24 do not qualify for the refundable portion of the credit, it is important to review the regulations that apply to each case as there are several exceptions. Filing a joint return or when both parents are deceased are two cases where a student under age 24 could qualify. Students that are age 18 and over may also qualify if they provide more than half of their support through earned income, or if they are only attending part-time.

Recent proposals have suggested that the qualifying age be reduced to 21, so a review of current laws may be appropriate. Taxpayers can also use the IRS Interactive Tax Assistant at http://www.irs.gov/uac/Am-I-Eligible-to-Claim-an-Education-Credit%3F to see if they qualify.

Publication 970 provides these qualifications for the refundable part of the credit.

You **do not** qualify for a refund if items 1 (a, b, or c), 2, **and** 3 below apply to you.

1. You were:
    a. Under age 18 at the end of the tax year, **or**
    b. Age 18 at the end of the tax year **and** your earned income (defined below) was less than one-half of your support (defined below), **or**
    c. Over age 18 and under age 24 at the end of the tax year **and** a full-time student (defined below) **and** your earned income (defined below) was less than one-half of your support (defined below).
2. At least one of your parents was alive at the end of the tax year.
3. You are filing a return as single, head of household, qualifying widow(er), or married filing separately.

It is important to notice the ands and ors, and verify any information to the contrary. It may be more useful if the qualifications show who does qualify. Changing some terms and the ands and ors, you may be able to use the following alternate outline.

You DO qualify for a refund if items 1 (a, b, or c), 2, **or** 3 below apply to you.

1. You were:
    a. Age 18 at the end of the tax year **and** your earned income (defined below) was at least one-half of your support (defined below), **or**
    b. Over age 18 and under age 24 at the end of the tax year

and not a full-time student (defined below), **or**

   c. Over age 18 and under age 24 at the end of the tax year **and** your earned income (defined below) was at least one-half of your support (defined below), **or**

   d. At least age 24.

2. Neither of your parents was alive at the end of the tax year.
3. You are filing a joint return.

Note that the tax code defines those who do not qualify through a series of referrals. See IRC § 25A(i)(5) and references for specific details. The refundable credit is not available to a child to whom § 1(g) (Kiddie tax) applies, which refers to § 152(c)(3). Although § 152(c)(3) includes simply a student under 24, the definition of student in this section is a full-time student as defined in § 152(f)(2)(A).

Fortunately dependency rules may avoid having to make the determination since the credit cannot be claimed if the student doesn't claim his own exemption. Unfortunately, it's possible that neither the taxpayer nor the student can claim the refundable portion of the credit. If the student provides more than half of his own support through unearned income, he cannot be claimed as a dependent, but since the support is not through earned income he might not be able to claim the refundable portion of the credit. Furthermore, since the credit is divided into refundable and nonrefundable, he cannot get the full credit even if tax liability was more than $2,500.

Flowcharts
The following flowcharts can assist in determining eligibility.

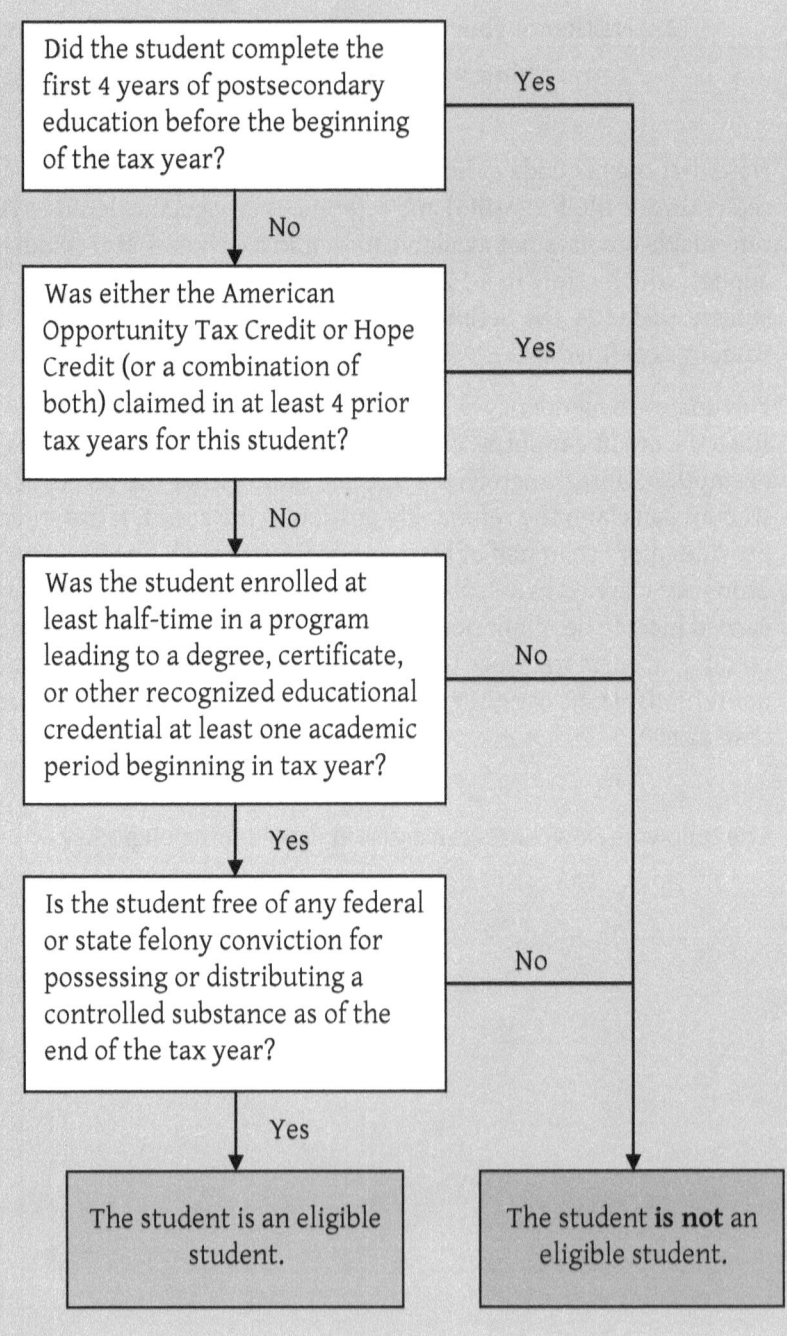

American Opportunity Tax Credit Student Qualifications Test

Did the student complete the first 4 years of postsecondary education before the beginning of the tax year?

Yes

No

Was either the American Opportunity Tax Credit or Hope Credit (or a combination of both) claimed in at least 4 prior tax years for this student?

Yes

No

Was the student enrolled at least half-time in a program leading to a degree, certificate, or other recognized educational credential at least one academic period beginning in tax year?

No

Yes

Is the student free of any federal or state felony conviction for possessing or distributing a controlled substance as of the end of the tax year?

No

Yes

The student is an eligible student.

The student **is not** an eligible student.

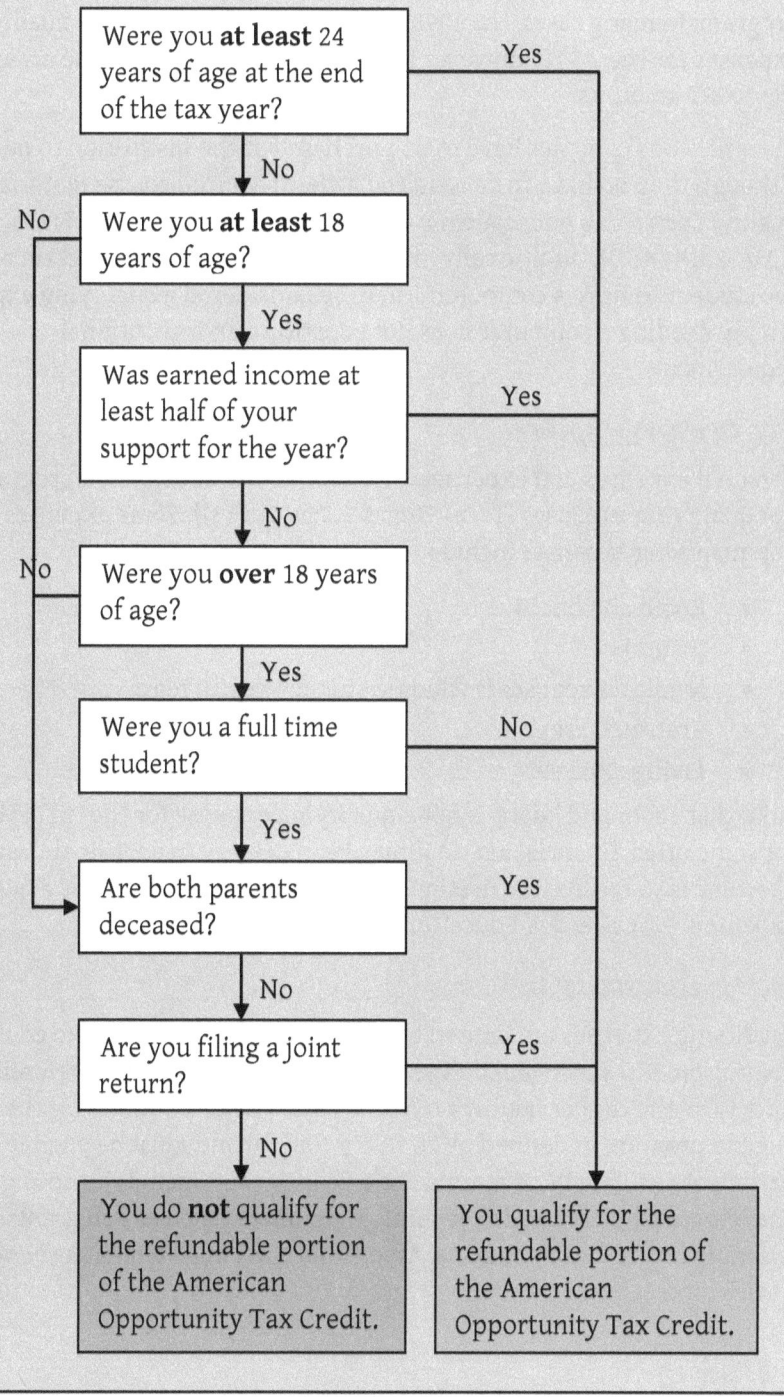

Qualifying Expenses

Qualifying expenses define what can be claimed for the AOTC. Expenses that can be used to claim the credits include costs of tuition and required fees, as well as required books and course materials. They do not include fees paid for sports, games, or hobbies unless the courses are required for the degree program. In many cases, the 1098T will provide the amount of qualifying expenses for the AOTC; however the preparer should verify the accuracy of the 1098T amounts.

Currently books do not have to be purchased at the institution to qualify although they do have to be required. Other required course materials also qualify. Even some nonacademic expenses may be qualifying (Treas. Reg. § 1.25A-2(d)(2)(iii)). Additionally, if an institution or degree program requires the student to have a computer it may be considered a qualifying expense. Simply needing a computer does not constitute an institutional requirement.

Non Qualifying Expenses

Personal expenses and expenses unrelated to the educational program are not qualifying expenses (Treas. Reg. § 1.25A-2(d)(3)). Some expenses that are not qualifying expenses include

- Room and board
- Insurance
- Medical Expenses (including student health fees)
- Transportation
- Living expenses

Note that room and board is not a qualifying expense for the AOTC, but it is for some other financial aid, so it may be necessary to coordinate with other allowances to receive the maximum benefit. Room and board is a qualifying expense for a Coverdell Educational Savings Account.

Eligible Educational Institution

Qualifying expenses are limited to tuition and fees at an eligible educational institution. IRC § 25A(f)(2) defines the eligible programs with reference to Title IV of the Higher Education Act of 1965. The institution must be an eligible program as defined by 20 USC § 1088(b) and must be eligible to participate in Title IV programs. Title IV programs include various grants and loans authorized by the federal government, such as Pell grants and federally insured student loans. An on-line class in an eligible program does qualify.

In addition to having qualifying expenses, the taxpayer must have made payments for those expenses in tax year. Payments for qualifying expenses include amounts paid by the student, or by the taxpayer, or paid through student loans. Payments can be made by cash or credit. All expenses can be claimed by taxpayers that claim the student as an exemption on their tax return (Treas. Reg. § 1.25A-5(a)).

Payments made by a third party that are in the nature of a gift are also qualifying as paid by the taxpayer. So if a grandparent pays the institution for part of the cost of attending college, the taxpayer can claim the credit using those amounts. The code defines third party expenditures with the phrase, "directly to an eligible educational institution to pay for a student's qualified tuition and related expenses" (Treas. Reg. § 1.25A-5(b)). IRS Publications, however, do not include the restriction that third party payments are made to the institution. Also included in amounts considered paid by the taxpayer are certain scholarships that the taxpayer includes in income. This is discussed in detail later.

The school term for which expenses are paid is also important. Generally payments must be made in the year the term begins. There is one exception. If the payments are made for qualifying expenses for the first three months of the following year, they can be considered as qualifying in the year paid. Payments made in the tax year after the *beginning* of the school term are not qualified payments (Treas. Reg. § 1.25A-5(e)). For example, if the term begins in December, payments made in the following year do not qualify for that term, even if it ends in the following year.

Note: A special rule applies to qualified installment agreements which could delay the recognition of payments for purposes of claiming education credits (Treas. Reg. § 1.25A-5(e)(4)). Tax preparers should review the terms of the agreement to determine when the payments are considered paid and if they qualify as being paid in the tax year. Payments made through student loans are considered paid when the expenses have been paid by the loan originator.

Lifetime Learning Credit

The LLC is similar to the AOTC in that qualifying expenses are required, but the credit is not refundable. The LLC credit amount is only 20% of expenses. Other differences also exist. Whether you use the LLC or decide to take a deduction may depend on your marginal tax rate as well as MAGI. The credit is phased out for modified MAGI between $52,000 ($104,000 joint), and $62,000 ($124,000 joint).

Qualifications

The LLC does not have as stringent student qualifications. While it must be at an eligible educational institution, it does not require the student to be seeking a degree credential (Treas. Reg. § 1.25A-4(c)). The expenses can be used to pay for expenses as part of a postsecondary degree program or to simply help the student to acquire or improve a job skill. The LLC does not require half-time attendance and isn't limited by a drug felony conviction. Up to $10,000 of expenses can be considered in calculating the credit (IRC § 25A(c)). The taxpayer can take the credit for an unlimited number of years.

Qualifying Expenses

Qualifying expenses for the LLC include costs of tuition and required fees, as well as required books. The inclusion of "course materials" is an AOTC specific allowance (IRC § 25A(i)(3), but there is no clear definition of course materials in the code. According to IRS publications, though, books DO have to be required and purchased at the institution to be qualified expenses. Other expenses are qualifying if required to be paid to the institution as a condition of enrollment or attendance. Expenses can also be prepaid for the first three months of the following year.

Deductions

Tuition and Fees Deduction

A deduction for educational expenses is also available to taxpayers. The deduction lowers the amount of taxable income. The student requirements are similar to the requirements for a credit, although the expense restrictions are similar to the LLC. The code refers to the definition of qualified expenses provided in IRC § 25A(f), but includes only "qualified tuition and related expenses" (IRC § 222(d)(1)). According to IRS publications, all amounts must be paid to the institution as a condition of enrollment. In other words, if the student has the option of purchasing course materials elsewhere they are not deductible even if purchased from the institution (Publication 970).

Currently, taxpayers can take up to $4,000 deduction for tuition expenses (IRC § 222(b)(3)). Payments for qualifying expenses must be paid by the taxpayer or spouse. Payments made by dependents or third parties do not qualify. The expenses can be for undergraduate or graduate studies and the phase-out begins at $60,000 ($130,000 joint). The deduction is not available to taxpayers with MAGI over $80,000 ($160,000 joint).

Deciding between this deduction and the LLC will depend on differences in qualifying expenses, payments, treatment of dependent scholarships, and the taxpayer's marginal tax rate. If the taxpayer is in the 25% tax bracket, the deduction is the equivalent of a 25% tax credit on the same amount, although there could be some side effects related to a difference in AGI. The EITC could be affected by excluding tuition expenses from AGI.

Benefit Comparison

The IRS provides a summary comparison of these three benefits at http://www.eitc.irs.gov/Other-Refundable-Credits/educompchart. There are several other benefits that can be used when considering educational expenses and taxation.

Business Deduction for Work-Related Education

A related deduction for education expenses required for work can be claimed as an itemized deduction. Although it doesn't require attendance at an eligible institution, there are rules concerning what qualifies as work-related. You can deduct the cost of qualifying work-related education as a business expense if it meets these two tests

- The education is required by your employer or the law to keep your present salary, status or job. The required education must serve a bona fide business purpose of your employer.
- The education maintains or improves skills needed in your present work.

AND

- It is **not** needed to meet the minimum educational requirements of your present trade or business or
- It is **not** a part of a program of study that will qualify you for a new trade or business.

This may be considered a last resort deduction, since the rules are so complex and it requires itemizing deductions. Expenses for books, supplies, certain transportation, travel, and other necessary expenses can be included.

The deduction must be claimed on Schedule A of an individual return for employees or on a business schedule (Schedule C or Schedule F) for a self-employed person. On Schedule A, expenses are subject to the 2% floor. Reimbursements must be treated according to "accountable plan" rules.

Employer-Provided Educational Assistance

Another benefit is the Employer-Provided Educational Assistance program. When qualifying benefits are provided to employees, the value of the benefits may not be taxable. Education generally includes any form of instruction or training that improves or develops your capabilities. The payments do not have to be for work-related courses or courses that are part of a degree program. The benefit is limited to $5,250 and is excluded from taxable wages on a W-2. Excess amounts are taxable.

No Double Benefit

One of the most important concepts in tax law is "no double benefit." If you claim one benefit, you are generally restricted from claiming a related benefit. For example, you can't claim AOTC and LLC for the same student, nor can you take the tuition deduction for the same student. Similarly, scholarships can't be considered tax-free if the qualifying expenses are used to claim a tax credit or deduction.

Even though taxpayers can combine AOTC or LLC with some other tax benefits, the same expenses can't be used for more than one benefit. For example, while Section 529, Coverdell Savings Account, and some other tax benefits are generally tax-free, they are not tax-free if used to pay qualifying expenses used to claim an education credit. When multiple tax benefits are involved, understanding how to coordinate the various benefits can assist in maximizing the potential tax breaks.

General Scholarship Treatment

For both the AOTC and LLC, scholarships are often treated as tax-free when applied to qualified expenses, in which case the qualified expenses are reduced by that amount. The tax code defines the term *qualified scholarship* as any amount used for qualifying expenses refers to both scholarships and grants (IRC § 117(b)(1)). When scholarships are not considered qualified, or tax-free, they are included in the taxpayer's gross income. Similarly, scholarships in excess of qualified expenses are taxable, although some expenses may be qualified tax-free by other plans.

Scholarships (or fellowships) that are paid for services rendered to the institution are not tax-free scholarships and should always be included in income. This might include scholarships that require student teaching or research assistance and would be reported to the taxpayer on a W-2. Some exceptions to this exclusion include the National Health Service Corps Scholarship, the Armed Forces Health Professions Scholarship (IRC § 117(c)), and Qualified Tuition Reduction (IRC § 117(d)).

While scholarships generally offset expenses, the regulations do allow taxpayers to treat some scholarships differently in order to increase their qualifying expenses. That is one of the primary reasons for this text and it is covered in the next section.

Regulations

The tax code in Internal Revenue Code Section 25A outlines the legal requirements (as passed by Congress) for education credits, but there are separate regulations that the IRS has released that define how they will treat education credits and qualifications. The regulations explain how taxpayers should report items for education credits. The regulations answer questions that taxpayers may have concerning the law itself. Very often, regulations include examples of treatment.

For example, IRC § 25A defines the Hope and Lifetime Learning Credits. IRC § 25A(i) amends that section to include the American Opportunity Tax Credit. Treas. Reg. § 1.25A-1 through Treas. Reg. § 1.25A-5 are the Internal Revenue regulations that cover the law in IRC § 25A. In most cases, taxpayers can rely on treasury regulations in reporting their taxes. One of the regulations, Treas. Reg. § 1.25A-5 enhances/clarifies the options taxpayers have when claiming education credits, allowing them to coordinate their benefits to achieve the greatest advantage.

The regulations do provide examples and explanations that can be useful for tax preparers. However, the Treasury Directive (TD 9034) that contained the original regulations can also be useful in explaining other characteristics of the regulations, and answering comments and questions about the regulations.

Initial Regulations

The first four regulations cover the basic requirements for IRC § 25A by describing requirements and calculation of the credits (Treas. Reg. § 1.25A-1), definitions (Treas. Reg. § 1.25A-2), specific requirements for the Hope Credit (Treas. Reg. § 1.25A-3), and specific requirements for the Lifetime Learning Credit (Treas. Reg. § 1.25A-4). These are reflected in the description of the credits above. The last regulation related to IRC § 25A provides guidelines for coordinating scholarships and the expenses used to qualify for the credit.

Coordinating Scholarships and Grants to Maximize Credits

Entitled "Special rules relating to characterization and timing of payments," Treas. Reg. § 1.25A-5 gives the procedure for calculating expenses for the credit and outlines the rules for calculating the credit and in particular where scholarships and grants are involved.

In general, education credits are available for amounts that the taxpayer pays and scholarships are tax-free to the degree they are used for qualifying expenses. However, it may be possible to qualify for or increase the amount of both the AOTC and the LLC by including some scholarships and grants in income. This is largely dependent on the type of scholarship or grant.

IRC § 117 defines qualified scholarships as **any amount** of a scholarship used for qualified expenses and requires the qualified expenses for the credit to be reduced to reflect that tax-free nature. However some scholarships can be treated as taxable or non-taxable based on the terms of the scholarship as outlined in Regulation 1.25A-5(c)(3). The regulation also includes multiple examples illustrating the potential effects of considering scholarship taxable income. For tax purposes grants follow the same logic as scholarships and the IRS has recently focused on Pell grants in making this treatment more familiar.

Three Types of Scholarships

The tax code only describes taxable and qualified (or tax-free) scholarships, and qualified scholarships only describe amounts of a scholarship that are used to pay qualified expenses. In order to better understand the types of scholarships in regards to tax treatment, I define scholarships here as 1) exclusive, 2) taxable, or 3) elective. Briefly, exclusive scholarships cover only qualified expenses, taxable scholarships cover non-qualified expenses, and elective scholarships may be used to cover qualified or non-qualified expenses. Although not defined as such in the code, the three types are covered in IRC § 117(b)(1) and Treas. Reg. § 1.25A(c)(3). The elective nature of the third type is what enables us to re-allocate scholarship amounts effectively increasing qualified expenses to achieve the highest credit amount.

Exclusive Scholarships

Exclusive scholarships are those scholarships, by the terms of scholarship, which must be used to pay qualified expenses. The full amount of the scholarships must reduce the amount of qualified expenses. Because the scholarship must be used for qualified expenses, no amount should be refunded. In some cases scholarships terms determine the amount of the scholarship based on the amount of qualified expenses, but that may not indicate that the funds must be used for those expenses. The Louisiana TOPS case, later, describes such a scenario. Still, the conservative treatment is to consider scholarships exclusive until determined otherwise.

Taxable Scholarships

A scholarship that **must be used** exclusively for **other than** qualified expenses is taxable. It is reported on line 7 as scholarship income with other taxable scholarships. Room and board is not a qualifying expense, so scholarships that cover only that is *normally* taxable. Scholarships in excess of qualifying expenses are also treated as taxable scholarships. As you will see next, some scholarships can be **treated** as taxable scholarships.

A scholarship that pays students for services they must perform, such as teaching or research, are generally taxable and reported as earned income on a W-2. They should not enter into the calculation of education credits.

Elective Scholarships

The third type of scholarship is the elective scholarship. The term elective is not described in the code as such but the concept is taken from Treas. Reg. § 1.25A-5(c)(3) where scholarship amounts can be treated as either taxable or tax-free. The concept is also published in IRS Publication 970. The phrase that separates exclusive from elective in this context is "used for other than qualified expenses." If a scholarship **may** or **must** be used for other than qualified expenses you can elect to include it in income, or treat it as tax-free and offset qualified expenses. When treated as income, the amount of qualified expenses is not reduced and the taxpayer may qualify for a higher education credit.

Pell Grants

Scholarships that are available for elective treatment include Pell grants. In fact, determining if other scholarships are elective will often not be necessary. Pell grants may often be $4000 or more of the aid received by the student, the maximum amount considered in calculating the AOTC. The LLC expense limit is $10,000. Most other federal aid, as well as Coverdell Educational Savings Accounts and Section 529 accounts can also be treated as elective scholarships (IRC § 530(d)(2)(C)).

Measured Scholarships

Although there is no regulation that addresses scholarships that are "measured by" the amount of tuition, as opposed to "used for" tuition, IRS rulings do support the elective nature of such scholarships. While that may seem to be simply semantics, a change in the wording was the defining characteristic that allowed scholarship inclusion in the Louisiana TOPS program. Just because a scholarship is based on the costs of tuition does not mean it is limited to tuition costs. In an IRS private letter ruling (PLR) related to the Louisiana Tuition Opportunity Program for Students (TOPS) program in Louisiana, it was determined that the TOPS awards could be applied to Section 25A and 117 in determining tax treatment.[1]

---

[1] *www.irs.gov/pub/irs-wd/0137006.pdf* (PLR **200137006**)

In 1999 the Louisiana legislature went from a system that required a TOPS award to **be used** for tuition to a system that **measures** the amount of the award **by** the amount of tuition. In that program the amount of the scholarship is limited to the **amount** of tuition, and the IRS has determined that this scholarship qualifies to be included in income to increase QE for education credits.

Although PLRs cannot be used as precedent, the logic can be used to make the case for similar scenarios. The TOPS ruling confirms that (then proposed) Treas. Reg. § 1.25A-5(c)(3) allows this grant to be considered a "qualified scholarship excludable from income under section 117" unless:

> (i) The grant is reported as income on the taxpayer's federal income tax return, or

> (ii) The grant must be applied, by its terms, to expenses other than qualified tuition and related expenses within the meaning of section 117(b)(2), such as room and board."

Following the ruling, the Louisiana Law Review published an article encouraging recipients of the TOPS grant to consider using Treasury Reg. 1.25A-5 to amend their returns to claim education credits.[2]

Following are excerpts from the PLR

> 4. *Federal tax consequences of the Louisiana TOPS Award under §§ 25A and 117.*

> *As noted earlier, prior to being amended in 1999, Louisiana law required that awards made to students under the TOPS program be spent on tuition. As such, the amount of any award was excludable from gross income under § 117 and reduced the amount of qualified expenses eligible for the education tax credit. However, in 1999, the Louisiana legislature amended the TOPS statute for the express purpose of qualifying a student or his parent or guardian for the § 25A credit. The legislature amended the TOPS statute to –*

> *(1) provide that TOPS awards are in an amount equal to tuition (rather than being for tuition);*

2

http://digitalcommons.law.lsu.edu/cgi/viewcontent.cgi?article=5806&context=lalrev

(2) cause the administering agency to direct the institution that whenever the TOPS award is paid on behalf of the student and the student's tuition is paid from a source other than the TOPS award, the award is to be applied by the educational institution toward payment of those "costs of attendance" other than tuition; and

(3) permit a student to elect to defer receipt of a TOPS award and to spend the amount received on costs of attendance other than tuition and provide that the amount of the award will be reduced if a § 25A credit is claimed.

..

We view these statutory provisions as terms of the grant and discuss below the effect the Service should give these terms in applying §§ 25A and 117 to award recipients.

..

Under the terms of the grant as we construe them, therefore, the Service should give effect to Louisiana's changes under (1), above, which permit the award to be used for either qualifying or non-qualifying expenses. Under this interpretation, the exclusion of the grant is determined by the tax reporting of the grantee.

The terms of the Texas Grant now contains similar wording and may be considered elective in the same manner as the TOPS. As more taxpayers take advantage of Regulation 1.25A-5(c)(3), the IRS may issue other regulations clarifying what constitutes elective scholarships.

On the other hand, the Texas Hazlewood Exemption for Texas veterans would not be considered elective because of its strict regulation that amounts are for tuition and required fees, and because it is an exemption rather than an amount provided to the taxpayer.

Other Elective Scholarships

If it's necessary to consider the elective nature of other scholarships research will be required, but that research outlay can be used on multiple returns. A practitioner that researches area scholarships in advance can quickly answer questions about the elective nature of particular scholarships. A repository of information related to these scholarships will be invaluable during tax season. Finding out if scholarships can be taxable can be a formidable task, however. The section on Research may help in that endeavor.

Dual Requirements

In some cases, scholarships may be required to be used for a combination of qualifying and non-qualifying expenses, for example, only tuition and room and board. These scholarships would be partially exclusive and partially elective. If that is the case, the amount must be allocated between the two amounts.

One of the IRS scenarios in Treas. Reg. § 1.25A-5 explains the treatment of such scholarships and it is discussed later when illustrating the use of the AOTC worksheet.

Lifetime Learning Credit

Although the focus has been on the AOTC, elective scholarships can be treated the same way in calculating the LLC. There are differences in what constitutes qualifying expenses, however. The most notable exception is that books must have been purchased from the institution and may already be included on the 1098T. The LLC would apply, for example, if the student has already received his 4-year degree before the beginning of the tax year, or was not attending at least half-time. The LLC is not refundable.

Research

The most challenging aspect of preparing tax returns for clients claiming education credits which include scholarships in income is determining what scholarships are elective. It's not a difficult task for most federal grants, but it can be particularly challenging for locally funded scholarships. Following are examples of scholarships that I have determined to be elective, from federal to state and local. Rather than rely on calls and letters to local colleges, I did most of the research on the Internet.

All of the circumstances should be weighed when determining if a scholarship, grant, or other source is evaluated for possible treatment as an elective scholarship suitable for maximizing the education credits. However, some key words to look for are "room and board", "living expenses", "housing", and "excess refunded". While "excess refunded" is not a key term for IRS rules, it is a good indicator. It is important that a review of the terms do not require that certain costs be paid for with the scholarships.

Federal Grants

Federal grants are a common source of financial aid. Most federal aid, including the Pell Grants, are need-based, and since the term "need" includes food and a place to stay, you might conclude that they may be used for other than qualified expenses. You don't have to wrangle with that. The federal student aid website provides this Q&A.

Q6. What costs does a Federal Pell Grant cover?

A6. Federal Pell Grants are available if you are taking classes as part of a program that leads to an undergraduate degree or certificate. Federal student aid, including Pell Grants, can be used to cover a variety of costs, generally including

Tuition and fees normally assessed;

Books, supplies, transportation, and miscellaneous personal expenses;

Living expenses such as room and board; and

An allowance for costs expected to be incurred for dependent care for a student with dependents.[3]

---

[3] http://federalstudentaid.ed.gov/opportunity/questions.html, Accessed 3/25/2014.

The IRS and the Treasury Department have specifically promoted the inclusion of Pell grants in income to qualify for education credits.

State Scholarships

TSBPA

The Texas State Board of Public Accountability (TSBPA) Fifth-Year Accounting Student Scholarship was one that applied to me in the past and I found this line on the TSBPA website that describes the uses for the award:

> The award may be used at a participating college or university in Texas that is recognized by the Board. The award may be used for tuition, fees, books, supplies, and living expenses incurred by the student in connection with the student's fifth year of an accounting program.[4]

Although this scholarship covers expenses for a five-year degree, it doesn't change the requirements for the AOTC. However, if the student has not "earned" a bachelor's degree **before** the **beginning** of the tax year he may still meet the requirements for AOTC even though he is taking graduate level classes.

TEXAS Grant

The TEXAS Grant terms are similar to the terms of the Louisiana TOPS program that measures the amount of the grant by the amount of the tuition and fees. As such, it would likely be considered eligible for the same treatment. The promotional website contains the following

> *The maximum award amount (including state and institutional funds) is equal to the student's tuition and required fees.*

That wording and the lack of related restrictions in the supporting regulation suggests that you can include it in income in order to increase education credits.

Local Research Examples

There are also official representations of the terms of several popular scholarships in Tyler institutions' websites.

---

[4] http://www.tsbpa.state.tx.us/scholarship/awards-uses-for-the-award.html, Accessed 3/25/2014.

UT Tyler

In most of the endowed UT Tyler scholarships, the first item describing the requirements is "Award may be used for the payment of tuition, fees, books and supplies at UT Tyler only." and then there is an addition that "Any remaining funds will be disbursed on the published financial aid disbursement date." If you apply logic, it seems to allow you to use remaining funds for personal expenses, and thus it may be used for other than qualified expenses. Fortunately, you don't have to twist any words here either. The UT Tyler Scholarship FAQ page confirms:

> Q: Will scholarship awards apply to tuition, fees, books, supplies, and housing?
>
> A: Yes, up to the value of the award.
>
> Q: If I have monies left over on my account after everything is paid, will I get those monies?
>
> A: Yes... Remaining funds will be refunded....[5]

Since the scholarship can be used for housing, it would clearly fit the mold for elective treatment. I suspect such elective scholarships are more common today because institutions don't want to keep track of whether you use the resources for qualified expenses. Everything is grouped together in the student's account, tuition and fees are paid, and the excess is refunded. However, it is best to find something that indicates a scholarship is elective.

Faulconer Scholarship

Another local scholarship available at Tyler Junior College is the Faulconer Scholarship. Faulconer Scholarships are awarded to African-American or Hispanic high school students who are graduating seniors living within the Tyler Junior College Tax District. The home page for the scholarship describes the qualifications and answers questions concerning the use of the scholarship. While the scholarship amounts may change depending on other aid the use of the funds meets the description of an elective scholarship.

> *What can the scholarship be used for?*
>
> *Your scholarship funds should be used to pay any regular educational fees at college, such as books, tuition, fees, supplies or meal tickets, room and board if needed. If, at the end of the year, you have not spent all of your scholarship funds, you may receive a refund from your college account.*

---

[5] http://www.uttyler.edu/scholarships/faq.php, Accessed 3/25/2014.

Unless you spend the refunded money toward your college expense, you may be subject to income tax on the balance refunded to you.[6]

Aid Designed for Scholarship Inclusion

While tax professionals should not assume all scholarships can be treated as elective, it appears that institutions and agencies are designing financial aid in order to avoid that aid being a barrier to claiming education credits. In some cases, managing the scholarships for qualifying expenses may just be too much trouble for the institutions. Many scholarships allow a refund of amounts not used. In other cases, guidelines are being changed to actually allow students to maximize the education credits. The TOPS case is one such instance, and the Texas Grant is also structured to allow scholarship inclusion using the same type of wording.

Given the tax law knowledge and research information, the next steps involved in claiming an education credit can be summarized as

- Document Preparation – accessing records of expenses and payments
- Student Account Tabulation – totaling the expenses and payments
- Tax Credit Calculation – calculating the maximum credit

---

[6] http://faulconerscholars.org/?page_id=83

Document Preparation

Claiming an education credit starts with preparing the information to be used to claim the credit. Accessing and organizing records to calculate the education credit is essential to preparing accurate returns. The biggest issue related to claiming education credits is acquiring records for education expenses. Not only are they needed to calculate the credit, document preparation is also important because the information forms the basis for documentation should the IRS request it.

Very often, other than a 1098T, the taxpayer does not provide records to support their education credit. While it is possible to ask them to provide those records, it may be more practical to guide them in accessing the records or access them yourself. Although institutions provide better access to student financial records in this digital age, some are not easily obtained. The local university, for example, can show the amounts paid but the software doesn't support printing a complete list of transactions from the website unless they are visible on screen. The most difficult situations are where the scholarships cover expenses and the institution does not provide students with the 1098T.

This simple guide is provided to assist in gathering the information needed to determine if the taxpayer qualifies for an education credit. This includes a description of the 1098T first and later includes instructions for getting educational expense information from two of the local colleges, UT Tyler and Tyler Junior College. Practitioners not in the Tyler area may want to create their own guide for accessing account information from colleges and universities in that area. Instructions for accessing prior year tax return information for amending returns is also provided later.

While this can be used by taxpayers to prepare information the preparer can use, practitioners may just want to have the client log into the account or provide the login information and then access, copy, and format the data themselves. That would alleviate some of the taxpayer's frustration and possibly avoid time-consuming errors. Generally, I ask the taxpayers who come in to the office to login to their account and I then copy the information to a spreadsheet where I can properly evaluate the expenses.

1098-T

Not Always Provided
The first item that should be reviewed and added to the documentation for education credits is a copy of the 1098T, if the institution provided one. Institutions are not required to release a 1098T if financial aid covers all of

the expenses (Treas. Reg. § 1.6050S-1(a)(2)(iii)). If that is the case, don't waste time waiting for one to come in the mail. I am told that the local university, UT Tyler, now provides 1098Ts to all students, while Tyler Junior College does still limit them to students with expenses greater than scholarships and grants.

Although the following statement appears on the most current TJC website, it is not true. Remember that students have the option of including some scholarships in income in order to qualify for tax credits.

> It's tax time! 1098T forms have been mailed to students who qualify for the tuition tax credit.

> How do I know if I qualified for the tax credit and if I am eligible to receive this form?

> Did you have financial aid or scholarships?

> Did you receive a refund of financial aid (excluding student loans)?

> If you answered yes to both of the above questions, more than likely you did not qualify to receive the tax form as you were not out of pocket to pay for your tuition and fees.

> Please check online at www.1098t.com to see if there is a form available for you. If nothing comes up, then you more than likely did not qualify and will not be receiving the form. For more information on whether or not you qualify for the tax credit, please see the website.

> It is the practice and policy of Tyler Junior College to only mail forms to students who qualify to claim the tax credit when filing their income tax.

Unfortunately similar advice can be found on many other college websites at this writing.

Not Required
The fact that a student doesn't receive a 1098T is confusing to taxpayers. Taxpayers should understand that not receiving a 1098T doesn't limit their ability to claim a credit. Many students may be missing out on the AOTC for this reason alone.

Not Enough Information
Even if you have the 1098T, in many cases the 1098T doesn't provide enough information. Although the IRS requires some institutions to provide students with a 1098-T showing expenses and aid received, and Form 8863 provides areas to enter the amounts, IRS instructions include the

admonition to verify the accuracy of 1098-T amounts. That admonition should be heeded because 1098-T amounts may often be inaccurate.

It's true that the 1098T can provide information you can use to calculate the credit, but those situations are limited. The most informative 1098T is one in which qualifying expenses are reported in box 1 and there is no check in box 7. If there is an amount given for scholarships taxpayers can take the difference and find either net qualifying expenses (if expenses are greater than scholarships) or excess scholarships. This doesn't, however, maximize the credit for the taxpayer if some of the scholarships are Pell grants or similar scholarships.

Boxes

Also potentially confusing to both taxpayer and preparer are the various ways in which amounts can be reported on a 1098T. The key items on a 1098T are

> Box 1 – Payments received for qualified tuition and related expenses
> Box 2 – Amounts billed for qualified tuition and related expenses
> Box 5 – Scholarships or grants
> Box 7 – Indicates expenses billed for January – March of the following year
> Box 8 – Indicates at least half-time student
> Box 9 – Indicates a graduate student

The two most commonly reported amounts on a 1098T are the expenses in Box 1 or Box 2, and the scholarships and grants reported in Box 5. If those are the only items on the 1098T then the taxpayer can generally calculate the credit from that and information about the nature of the scholarships.

If box 2 is used instead of box 1, you need to verify that billed amounts were actually paid and if all amounts paid were included in the amount billed.

Amounts Include Following Year

The most challenging forms are those with a check in Box 7, since that indicates some items billed are for the following year. Often institutions bill students in November or December for the spring semester. If scholarships and grants are involved these amounts may likely not be paid in the tax year.

Also, if box 7 is checked in the current year it is likely that the prior year 1098T included amounts billed in that year (not the tax year) but which are paid in the current tax year. So, box 2 amounts billed may not include all amounts paid in the tax year.

Research is necessary in this case. The preparer or client should review the student's financial account records for the correct amounts.

Advanced Payments

If amounts billed for the following year are actually paid, then the taxpayer can get a credit for that amount. For qualified expenses on record in December, but for the school term beginning in January of the following year, the payments will be qualified in the year paid. Note, however, that amounts paid in a prior year can only be claimed in that prior year, in line with Treas. Reg. 1.25A-5(e)(2), and if the payment is for expenses in the first three months of the following year. Current payments for prior year expenses do not qualify.

Qualified Expenses for What?

Even when a 1098T includes what appears to be the correct amount of qualifying expenses paid, it would be wise to also evaluate that from the actual student expenses. The instructions for preparing a 1098T are not specific when identifying qualifying expenses and they differ depending on whether the benefit is AOTC, LLC, or a tuition deduction.

Graduate Student

A check in Box 9 (graduate student) does not necessarily disqualify a student from receiving the AOTC. One of the requirements of AOTC is that the student did not earn a bachelor's degree, but that test is made based on the beginning of the tax year, not the end of the tax year. If a student graduated in May, all expenses for the year qualify for the AOTC.

Adjustments and Corrections

If Box 4 or Box 6 has an amount provided then the taxpayer may need to file an amended return for the prior year. As in other circumstances, whether the taxpayer must amend the return will depend on whether they received a tax benefit (directly or indirectly) for the prior year. If the amendment does not change the tax due, generally no amendment is required.

Box 3 indicates that the method of reporting has changed in the current year. If the student had expenses in the prior year it will be necessary to evaluate that.

Box 10 should also be considered since any reimbursements will reduce the amount of qualifying expenses.

The 1098T in 2015

As part of the push to educate taxpayers about education credit regulations, there is a change in the 2015 version of the 1098T. On the instructions on the back of the 2015 1098T the IRS has provided this tip.

> ...
>
> **Box 5.** Shows the total of all scholarships or grants administered and processed by the eligible educational institution. The amount of scholarships or grants for the calendar year (including those not reported by the institution) may reduce the amount of the education credit you claim for the year.
>
> **TIP.** You may be able to increase the combined value of an education credit and certain educational assistance (including Pell Grants) if the student includes some or all of the educational assistance in income in the year it is received. For details, see Pub. 970.
>
> ...

Even with that change many students will not know that option if the institutions do not have to issue them a 1098T.

Accessing the 1098T

Institutions generally mail 1098T by the end of January of the tax year. In some cases, the form, or a link to it, may be provided through e-mail. If the student doesn't receive a 1098T they may be able to download one from the institution's website.

In some cases, the institution lets a third-party service handle the availability of 1098Ts on-line. A key provider for local colleges is at

www.1098t.com

Once you log in you may be shown a page

FORM 1098-T ELECTRONIC DELIVERY AUTHORIZATION

Students don't have to authorize electronic delivery. By authorizing electronic delivery, they will have future forms e-mailed to you instead of receiving paper forms in the mail. Instead, click on the Student Information in the left side panel, and select the year and school, and click "View My 1098T Tax Form." This will show a PDF download that you can save.

Whether or not taxpayers have a 1098T it is advisable to get the student's account information to clarify and verify the amounts. The student account will also typically show the name of the scholarship or grant and that can assist in determining if it is an elective scholarship or not.

Following are the procedures for accessing student account information from two of the local schools. Practitioners outside of this area may wish to document the procedures for colleges in their area.

UT Tyler

The myUTTyler website provides UT Tyler students with access to their accounts. Unfortunately, the site does not make it easy to download information on qualifying expenses. Although you can display detailed information, their system currently doesn't support printing that information. Instead, the system will only print the visible screen. This is one way to get the information that you need from their website if you do not have that information elsewhere. By copying the data from the page into a spreadsheet, it is easier to categorize and total relevant amounts for the calculations. The following was done using the Firefox browser.

Login

Go to your browser and enter

my.uttyler.edu

This will redirect to something that starts with *https://sis-portal-prod.uttyler.edu/psp/* and prompts the user to log in.

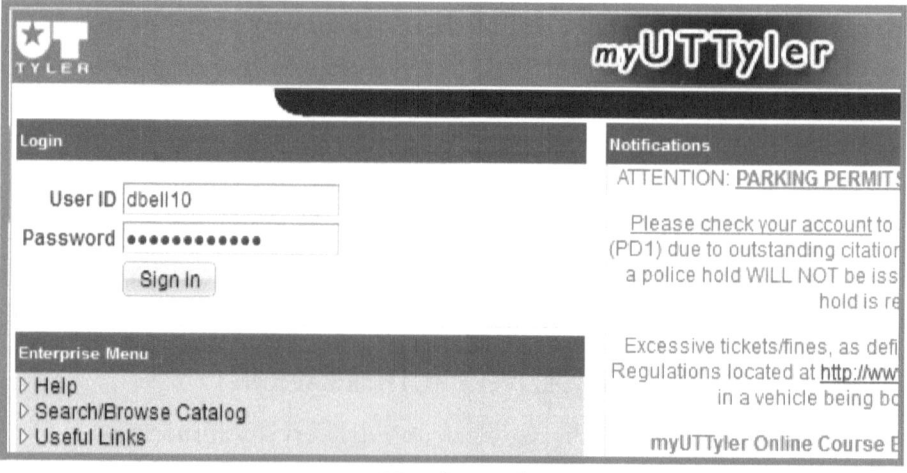

my UTTyler Login

Enter your User ID and password and click Sign In. Your UserID is normally the part of your patriots email address before the @ sign. Once you are in, you will see several items in the left menu

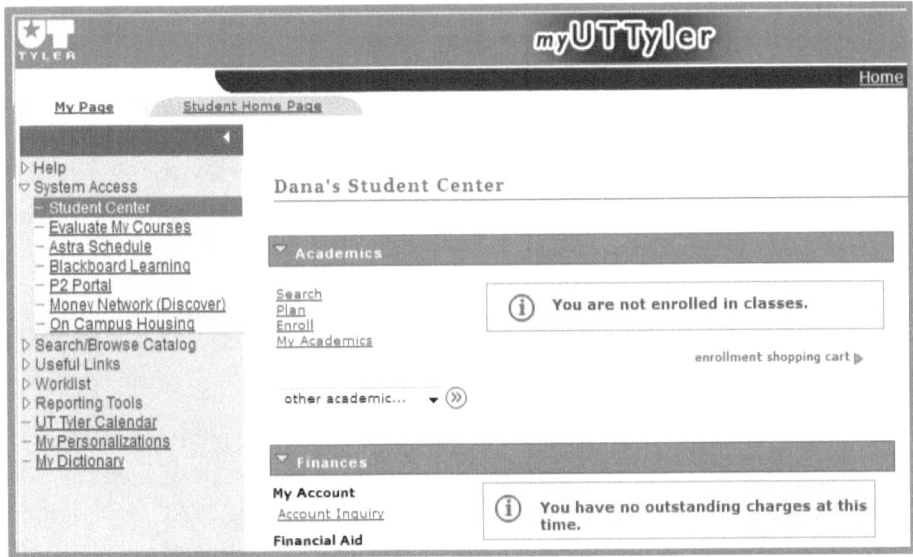

my UTTyler

Click on Student Access, then on Student Center, and under Finances, click Account Inquiry

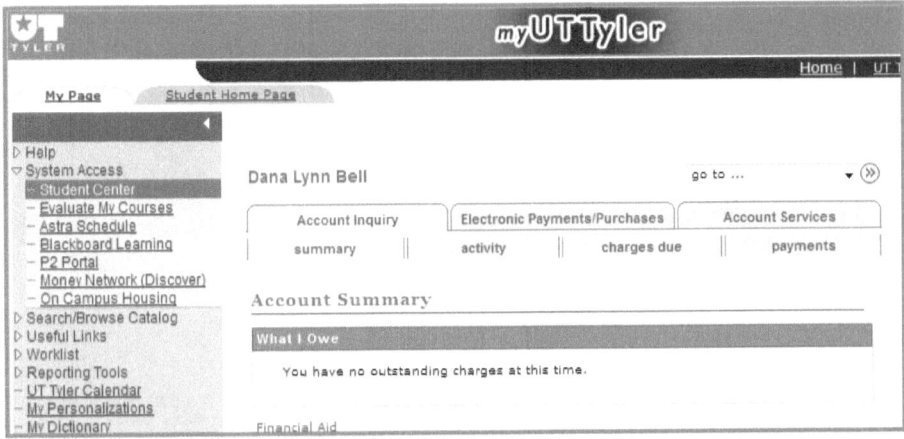

Account Inquiry

The display will then show several tabs at the top with Account Summary as the initial section shown. Click on the Activity sub-tab to select the transactions you will need.

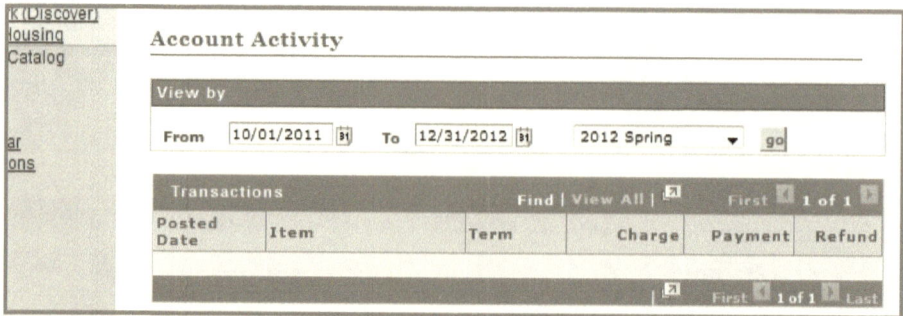

Account Activity

Under the subhead View by, select the dates you want to include in your inquiry. Ideally, enter the date three months before the start of the year, and then the end of the year. For 2014, the dates would be 10/01/2013 and 12/31/2014. Starting in the previous year is necessary because the University enters charges for Spring 2014 at the end of 2013.

Then select the term to report on, and press Go

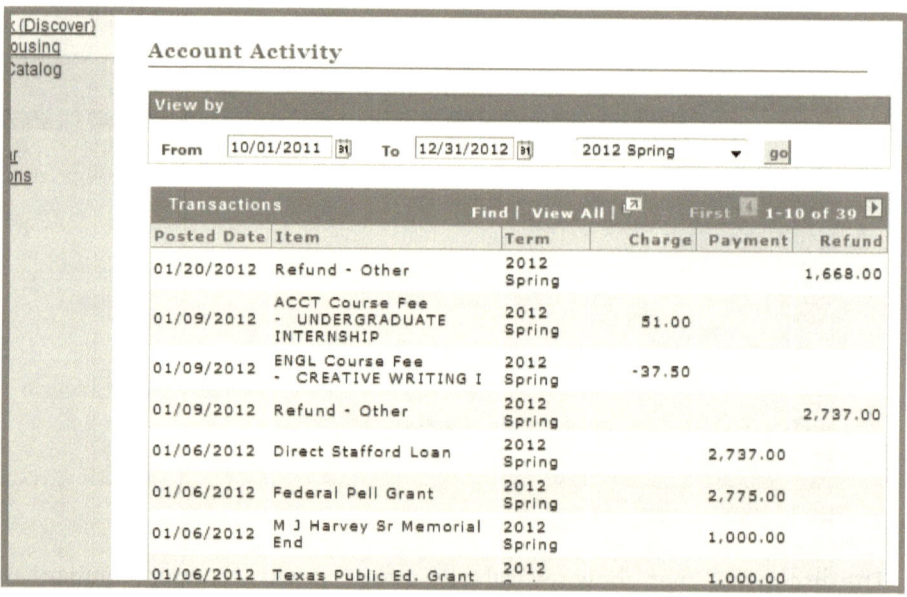

Term Inquiry

Initially the display will show only 10 lines at a time. Click on 'View All' in the table header to show all transactions (up to 100) for the term. If more than 100 items, you will have to display and process each 100 until complete.

Term Inquiry – All Items

What you do now will depend on what the tax preparer can work with. I haven't been able to print the complete list, so I copy and paste the information from the browser to Excel first.

Term Inquiry – Select Items

In order to copy/paste select the information on the page beginning to the left of Transactions head, mark all items in the table. Selecting is done by clicking, holding, and dragging to highlight the information you want. Right-click and select Copy.

Open Excel, select a cell, right-click and select paste. It will not look pretty at first but it can be fixed with a couple of steps.

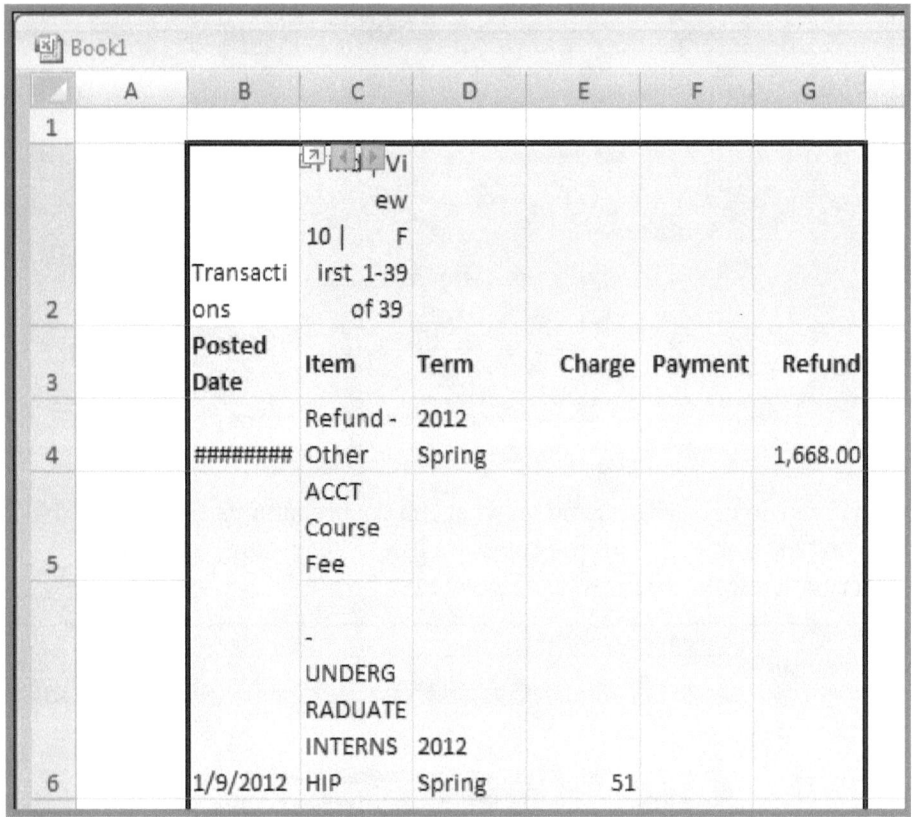

Excel – Paste Items

You may wish to repeat the copy/paste operation for each term before formatting the spreadsheet.

After you have copied the information into the spreadsheet you will need to reposition the columns and format for calculation.

The first step is to adjust the column widths to show all information. Click between the column headers and drag to widen the column to show the information without breaking words and obliterating the dates.

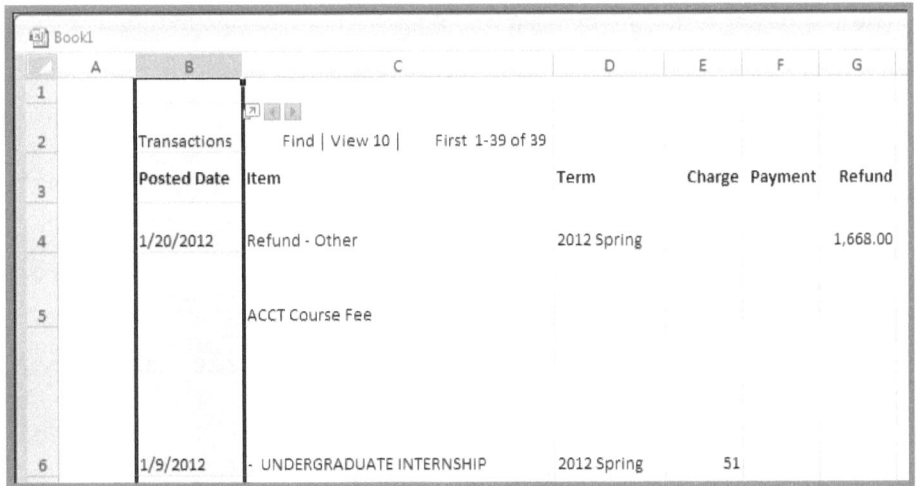

Excel – Column Adjustment

Next, select the entire worksheet by clicking in the top left corner.

Finally, adjust row heights by double clicking in the left column between two of the row headers. All rows should then by one or two lines high.

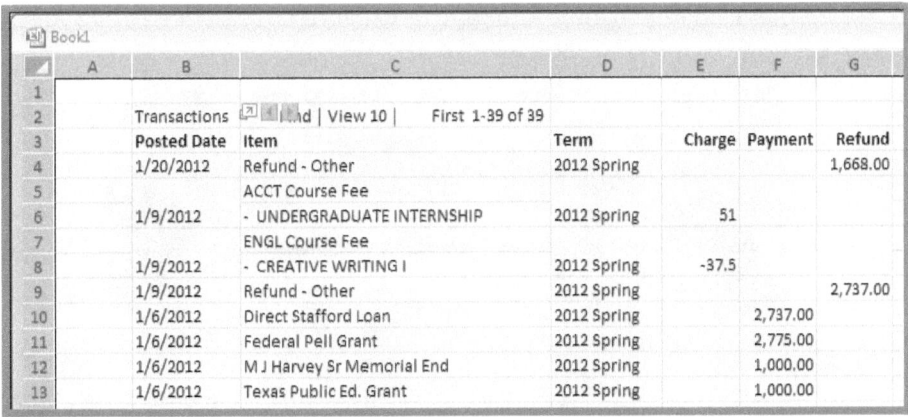

Excel – Row Adjustment

Repeat

Remember to repeat the Inquiry for each term attended. The information for separate terms does not have to be separate so you can append it to the previous data, or create separate sheets and generate a total for all terms. The site software does not have a way to select all terms in a particular tax year.

Be careful not to include amounts from terms in other years. Be careful not to omit amounts billed in other years that are paid in the tax year.

These spreadsheet(s) will be used in the next section to calculate the expenses.

Taxpayers can save and print the spreadsheets or bring the files to the tax preparer. The tax preparer can then evaluate the expenses and payments to see what qualifies for the education credit. Bringing spreadsheet files are better since he can more easily adjust the amounts to categorize and total the expenses, payments, and possible credit.

Tyler Junior College

TJC provides students easy access to their account from their home page.

Login

Go to your browser and enter **http://www.tjc.edu/**

TJC Quick Links

Students can log into their Apache Access account through Quick Links. Click on Quick Links and allow the page to expand the header showing the login window.

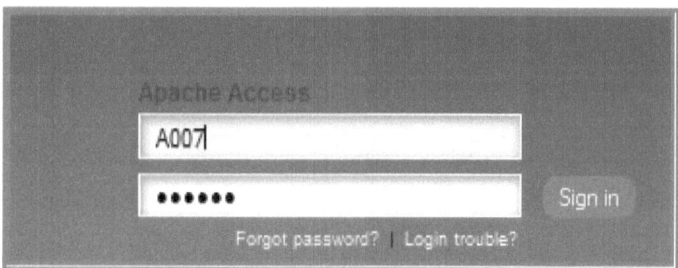

Apache Access - Login

Sign in using the students ID and password.

Apache Access

This will bring you to a site starting with *http://myapacheaccess.tjc.edu/*. Click on the Academics tab.

Inquiry

My Account

In the My Account box in the bottom right corner, select the term to view. Some financial data may be shown but you may need to select the more detailed information. Transactions should show dates, amounts, and description.

Payment History

At the bottom of the page click Statement and Payment History

Account Detail

At the bottom of the next screen, click Account Detail for Term

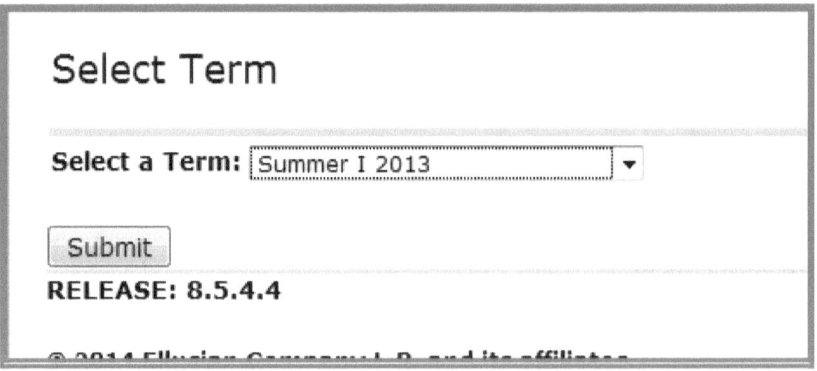

Select Term

Select a Term: Summer I 2013 ▼

Submit

RELEASE: 8.5.4.4

Select Term

201130 Summer I 2011 Term Detail					
Detail Code	**Description**	**Item Date**	**Charge**	**Payment**	**Balance**
DIST	Distance Education Fee	02-JUN-11	$15.00		
HLTF	Health Service Fee	02-JUN-11	$15.00		
LAB	Lab Fees	02-JUN-11	$25.00		
PARK	Parking Fee	02-JUN-11	$15.00		
REG3	Registration Fee	02-JUN-11	$25.00		
GNED	General Education Fee	02-JUN-11	$136.00		
STLF	Student Life Fee	02-JUN-11	$8.00		
TUI1	In-District Tuition	02-JUN-11	$112.00		
DIST	Distance Education Fee	02-JUN-11	-$15.00		
HLTF	Health Service Fee	02-JUN-11	-$15.00		
LAB	Lab Fees	02-JUN-11	-$25.00		
PARK	Parking Fee	02-JUN-11	-$15.00		
REG3	Registration Fee	02-JUN-11	-$25.00		
GNED	General Education Fee	02-JUN-11	-$136.00		
STLF	Student Life Fee	02-JUN-11	-$8.00		
TUI1	In-District Tuition	02-JUN-11	-$112.00		
HLTF	Health Service Fee	02-JUN-11	$15.00		
PARK	Parking Fee	02-JUN-11	$15.00		
REG3	Registration Fee	02-JUN-11	$25.00		
GNED	General Education Fee	02-JUN-11	$102.00		
STLF	Student Life Fee	02-JUN-11	$6.00		
TUI1	In-District Tuition	02-JUN-11	$84.00		
MCV	Mastercard/Visa Payment	12-MAY-11		$247.00	
	Net Term Balance				$0.00

Pay Now

TJC Term Detail

Then select the term to display the report for the applicable term. Select the items for the term, copy and paste into a spreadsheet. Other display options are available, but make sure dates and description are shown.

In some cases, as illustrated, fees are shown added and then subtracted for classes that are dropped from the original plan. Also note that the amounts in Charges must be categorized to total actual qualifying expenses as will be illustrated in the Calculations section.

Select another term at the bottom for other semesters to make further inquiries.

Student Account Tabulation

This section describes how to categorize and tabulate the relevant amounts. Although Treas. Reg. § 1.117-1 says you should exclude scholarships from income to the degree they are used for qualified expenses, Treas. Reg. § 1.25A-5(c) explains how you can manipulate some scholarships to increase the amount of qualified expenses you can use in calculating an education credit. The best way to determine the amounts to include in income requires some organization of expense and payment records.

Spreadsheet for Expense Calculations

While you can spend time verifying and adjusting the amounts on a 1098-T, taking a few minutes to get an account statement from the college will insure the taxpayer has an accurate record of amounts received and spent on qualifying expenses. Account records are usually accessible on-line by the student or parent claiming the education credit.

As described in the previous section, you may be able to mark, copy, and paste the amount from a web page into a spreadsheet. Some institutions may even have a way for students to export account information into a downloadable file. The following continues the example for UT Tyler given above.

Account Record

Date	Item	Term	Charge	Payment	Refund
12/9/2011	BIOL Course Fee - ANATOMY/PHYS...	2012 Spring	61		
12/9/2011	COSC Course Fee - INTERNET & WEB A..	2012 Spring	108		
12/9/2011	Designated Tuition - Undergrad	2012 Spring	2,476		
12/9/2011	Lab Fee - ANATOMY/PHYSIOLOGY LAB II	2012 Spring	5		
12/9/2011	Mandatory Fees - Fall/Spring	2012 Spring	915		
12/9/2011	Resident Tuition	2012 Spring	600		
12/9/2011	Student Services Fee	2012 Spring	132		
12/9/2011	Parking Permit Fall	2012 Spring	30		
12/21/2011	MANA Course Fee - DATABASE INFO S...	2012 Spring	49		
1/6/2012	Direct Stafford Loan	2012 Spring		2,737	
1/6/2012	Federal Pell Grant	2012 Spring		2,775	
1/6/2012	M J Harvey Sr Memorial End	2012 Spring		1,000	
1/6/2012	Texas Public Ed. Grant	2012 Spring		1,000	
1/9/2012	Refund - Other	2012 Spring			2,737
1/20/2012	Refund - Other	2012 Spring			399

In a student account there will usually be two or three columns, Charges, Payments, and possibly Refunds. Once the raw data is pasted into a spreadsheet, you can rename the existing columns to Qualified Expenses, Elective Scholarships, and Loans/Other. Between the first two amount columns, insert columns for Non-Qualified Expenses (the parking permit isn't qualified) and Exclusive Scholarships.

Add separate columns for Taxable Scholarships if applicable and move amounts to their appropriate column. Refund amounts can be grouped with student loans. In this example it is assumed all amounts have actually been paid so we are only categorizing expenses and scholarships. You may only need to move a few amounts as most will probably be qualifying expenses. When complete, add totals to the columns and use those amounts in the following worksheet.

Expense Spreadsheet

Date	Item	Term	Qual Exp	Non Qual	Excl Schps	Electve Schps	Loans/ Other
12/9/2011	BIOL Course Fee - ANATOMY/PHYS...	2012 Spring	61				
12/9/2011	COSC Course Fee - INTERNET & WEB..	2012 Spring	108				
12/9/2011	Designated Tuition - Undergrad	2012 Spring	2,476				
12/9/2011	Lab Fee - ANATOMY/PHYSIOLO L...	2012 Spring	5				
12/9/2011	Mandatory Fees - Fall/Spring	2012 Spring	915				
12/9/2011	Resident Tuition	2012 Spring	600				
12/9/2011	Student Services Fee	2012 Spring	132				
12/9/2012	Parking Permit Fall	2012 Spring		30			
12/21/2012	MANA Course Fee - DATABASE INFO..	2012 Spring	49				
1/6/2012	Direct Stafford Loan	2012 Spring					2,737
1/6/2012	Federal Pell Grant	2012 Spring				2,775	
1/6/2012	M J Harvey Sr Memorial End	2012 Spring				1,000	
1/6/2012	Texas Public Ed. Grant	Spring			1,000		
1/9/2012	Refund - Other	Spring					2,737
1/20/2012	Refund - Other	Spring					399
			4,346	30	1,000	3,775	5,873

Depending on the education credit you are claiming, be sure to add other qualifying expenses, such as required books and other course materials. This should be done even if you have $4,000 in educational expenses since they make that amount of remaining scholarships tax-free. If they are not purchased at the institution, you will have to add them manually.

When querying for the amounts for a school term, be sure to include several months before the start of the term since billing for the spring semester may begin in the previous year, and pay attention to what term the expenses are for. For example, the dates for Spring 2015 might include September 2014 – June 2015.

Expense amounts should be calculated on a term basis, including only terms that start in the tax year. Institutions typically use terms instead of tax years.

Tax Credit Calculation

There are three steps to the calculation of the education credit

1. Determine the amount of qualifying expenses
2. Determine the amount of taxable scholarships
3. Calculating the credit

The amounts are tabulated in the student's college account but must be reconciled to determine the net amount of qualifying expenses for the credit. That is the reason for the AOTC worksheet given below. The third step is primarily a software function, but it is important that preparers know how the 8863 calculations work.

In some cases, calculating the qualifying expenses is as easy as taking the amount in box 1 of Form 1098T, verifying that with the taxpayer and entering up to $4,000 of that amount on Form 8863. You could subtract scholarships from the box 1 amount and if the amount is $4,000 or more use that on Form 8863. Even when amounts from a Pell grant are included in income to maximize the credit, you can calculate that amount, add it to qualifying expenses and taxable scholarships, and no additional work may be required. That is illustrated in the TaxWise example later. It is when the amount of qualifying expenses is suspect, the calculations are more complex, or the nature of the scholarships is unknown that more work will be involved. For some of those situations you may be able to use the AOTC Worksheet in this section. If more than one type of scholarship was provided this worksheet may be a useful tool.

Calculating Expenses and Scholarships

The key amounts to calculate for education credits are qualifying expenses, scholarships, and the credit based on the net amount of expenses. If the relevant amounts have been exported and tabulated from the student account you can use the following worksheet to calculate the maximum credit amount and the amount of taxable scholarships if any.

Worksheet to Maximize Education Credits

The IRS does have a worksheet for calculating the education credit included in Pub 970 and other sources, but it is used to calculate what can be excluded from income and lacks the logic included in the regulations for elective taxable scholarships. The following worksheet can be used to aid in calculating the maximum AOTC amount. It can also be expanded or condensed to suit the needs of the practitioner.

This worksheet assumes the taxpayer does not have any outstanding balances, and does not consider other educational assistance, or the possibility of excluding qualified expenses of other types of financial aid. With more complex arrangements additional research and manipulation may be necessary.

Excel Formulas are given in the final column. If using a spreadsheet, you may want to include a process in your workflow to link the totals from the calculations to the appropriate cells in the spreadsheet. Notice that you only have to enter four amounts (if applicable) in the worksheet to calculate the amounts needed for the tax return. A self-calculating PDF version of the worksheet can be downloaded from www.tylerhosting.com/EdCredit/.

AOTC Worksheet

A	B	C	D	Formulas for Column D
1	Qualified Expenses	Enter the total amount of your qualified educational expenses.	4,346	
2	Total Scholarships	Enter the total amount of all scholarships and grants received for 2013.	4,775	
3	Taxable Scholarships	Enter the amount of scholarships **required to be used for other than** qualified expenses.	-0-	
4		Subtract line 3 from line 2.	4,775	=D2-D3
5	Excess Scholarships	If line 4 is greater than line 1, subtract line 1 from line 4.	429	=IF(D4>D1,D4-D1,0)
6	Potential Tax-free Scholarships	Subtract line 5 from line 4	4,346	=D4-D5
7	Exclusive Scholarships	Enter the amount of the scholarships that you are **required to use for** qualified educational expenses.	1,000	
8	Elective Scholarships	If line 6 is greater than line 7, Subtract line 7 from line 6.	3,346	=IF(D6>D7,D6-D7,0)
9	Excess Expenses Paid by Taxpayer	If line 1 is greater than line 6, Subtract line 6 from line 1	-0-	=IF(D1>D6,D1-D6,0)
10	Qualified Expenses for Tax Credit	Add line 8 and line 9 (maximum 4000). Enter this amount on **line 27 of Form 8863**.	3,346	=MIN(4000, D9+D8)
11	Elective Scholarships Includable in Income	If line 9 is less than line 10, subtract line 9 from line 10. Otherwise, enter 0.	3,346	=IF(D10>D9,D10-D9,0)
12	Total Scholarships Included in Income	Add line 3, line 5 and line 11. This is the amount of taxable scholarships. Enter SCH and this amount on the dotted line to the left of line 7. Include this amount in the total on **line 7 of Form 1040**.	3,775	=D3+D5+D11

The AOTC worksheet is only a tool and may not be enough for some circumstances. The preparer must understand the law to know what modifications may be needed for extraneous information. If Coverdell or Section 529 accounts are used you might be able to reduce qualifying expenses by the amount and continue with the worksheet. Not only is this worksheet useful for calculation it can be saved with the workpapers to document the calculation. In many cases, only a few numbers will be used in the calculations. Exclusive and taxable scholarships may never be a part of the computation.

Remember that scholarship amounts that cover services rendered such as teaching or research are normally considered taxable earned income, not scholarship income, and would not enter into the calculations.

IRS Scenarios

Following are scenarios illustrated in examples from Publication 970 and Treas. Reg. § 1.25A-5. The worksheet following demonstrates the use of the worksheet for these scenarios.

970-1: Bill Pass, age 28 and unmarried, enrolled full-time in 2013 as a first-year student at a local college to earn a degree in law enforcement. This was his first year of postsecondary education. During 2013, he paid $5,600 for his qualified education expenses and $4,400 for his room and board for the fall 2013 semester. He and the college meet all the requirements for the American opportunity credit. He figures his American opportunity credit based on qualified education expenses of $4,000, which results in a credit of $2,500.

970-3: The facts are the same as in *970-1*, except that Bill was awarded a $5,600 scholarship. Under the terms of his scholarship, it may be used to pay any educational expenses, including room and board. If Bill includes $4,000 of the scholarship in income, he will be deemed to have used that amount to pay for room and board. The remaining $1,600 of the $5,600 scholarship will reduce his qualified education expenses and his adjusted qualified education expenses will be $4,000. Based on his adjusted qualified education expenses of $4,000, Bill would be able to claim an American opportunity tax credit of $2,500.

25A-2: University X charges Student A, who lives on University X's campus, $3,000 for tuition and $5,000 for room and board. University X awards Student A a $2,000 scholarship. The terms of the scholarship permit it to be used to pay any of a student's costs of attendance at University X, including tuition, room and board, and other incidental expenses. University X applies the $2,000 scholarship against Student A's $8,000 total bill, and Student A pays the $6,000 balance of her bill from University X with a combination of savings and amounts she earns.

Student A reports the entire scholarship as income on the student's federal income tax return. Therefore, for purposes of calculating an education tax credit, Student A is treated as having paid $3,000 of qualified tuition and related expenses to University X.

25A-4: The facts are the same as in *25A-2*, except that the terms of the scholarship require it to be used to pay tuition or room and board charged by University X, and the scholarship amount is $6,000. Student A may allocate the scholarship between tuition and room and board in any manner. However, because room and board totals $5,000 that is the maximum amount that can be applied under the terms of the scholarship to expenses other than qualified expenses and at least $1,000 of the scholarship must be applied to tuition. If Student A reports $5,000 of the scholarship as income on the student's federal income tax return, then Student A will be treated as having paid $2,000 ($3,000 tuition–$1,000 qualified scholarship excludable under section 117) in qualified tuition and related expenses to University X.

			970-1	970-3	25A-2	25A-4
1	Qualified Expenses	Enter the total amount of your qualified educational expenses.	5600	5600	3000	3000
2	Total Scholarships	Enter the total amount of all scholarships and grants received for 2013.	0	5600	2000	6000
3	Taxable Scholarships	Enter the amount of scholarships **required to be used for other than** qualified expenses.				5000
4		Subtract line 3 from line 2.	0	5600	2000	1000
5	Excess Scholarships	If line 4 is greater than line 1, subtract line 1 from line 4.	0	0	0	0
6	Potential Tax-free Scholarships	Subtract line 5 from line 4	0	5600	2000	1000
7	Exclusive Scholarships	Enter the amount of the scholarships that you are **required to use for** qualified educational expenses.				1000
8	Elective Scholarships	If line 6 is greater than line 7, Subtract line 7 from line 6.	0	5600	2000	0
9	Excess Expenses Paid by Taxpayer	If line 1 is greater than line 6, Subtract line 6 from line 1	5600	0	1000	2000
10	Qualified Expenses for Tax Credit	Add line 8 and line 9 (maximum 4000). Enter this amount on **line 27 of Form 8863**.	4000	4000	3000	2000
11	Elective Scholarships Includable in Income	If line 9 is less than line 10, subtract line 9 from line 10. Otherwise, enter 0.	0	4000	2000	0
12	Total Scholarships Included in Income	Add line 3, line 5 and line 11. This is the amount of taxable scholarship. Enter SCH and this amount on the dotted line to the left of line 7. Include this amount in the total on **line 7 of Form 1040**.	0	4000	2000	5000

Understanding Form 8863

The lengthy form 8863 can be confusing, but the computations are really basic for most tax returns. Preparers will usually not need to use the form itself other than entering the qualifying expenses on page 2. The software usually does the rest. However, if the preparer reviews each page of the return with the taxpayer knowing how it works will be important.

The 8863 consists of two pages. As is often the case with IRS forms, page 2 is completed prior to completing page 1. There is only one 8863 per return, but if there are more than one student, there should be a page 2 of the form for each student showing student and institution information. It has four qualifications questions, qualifying expenses, and the initial calculation of the available credit. As the law directs, the credit is 100% of the first $2,000 and 25% of the second $2,000, and that is what the last section of part III calculates. This is the maximum credit allowed for your expenses.

The amounts from page 2 carry over to page 1 where the actual credit is calculated. There is a side calculation that adjusts for the phase-out. If line 6 is not a 1.000 then you can explain to the taxpayer that their credit is subject to the phase-out and explain the income levels being used. Then it calculates the refundable portion of the credit at 40% of the amount calculated at line 7. That is then subtracted from the line 7 amount to get the remainder which is the maximum nonrefundable credit portion. The nonrefundable portion is limited to taxable income after adjusting for a couple of other credits.

The education credit shows up on the 1040 on two separate lines. The nonrefundable credit shows in the credit section on the second page of Form 1040 (or variant) while the refundable credit shows in the payments section.

Phase-out Calculations
The completion of Form 8863 may be more involved if you are in the phase-out range for the AOTC. Tax software generally does that calculation but understanding how it is calculated may assist in deciding whether to and how much of scholarships to include in income. The phase-out is essentially based on percentage of income between lower and upper phase-out limits. Thus, $1000 over (based on $10,000 range) would reduce your credit by 10%.

If you happen to be put into the phase-out range by including scholarships and grants in income, re-calculate the credit omitting some or all of the scholarships to determine the most advantageous treatment. Generally, it will be most advantageous to include the first $2000 of expenses regardless of including scholarships in income. Above the first $2000, the net benefit will largely depend on your marginal tax rate, deductions, and the amount of tax owed.

Tax Preparation Techniques

Knowing how to process a particular return with potential education credits will save a considerable amount of time. In some cases you will not need to go to the trouble of completing a worksheet.

In many cases claiming the education credit for clients is relatively easy. If there are only taxpayer expenses you only need to determine the amount of qualifying expenses (QE). In many cases that is reported on the 1098T. Add required expenses paid elsewhere and the rest is math. It becomes just a little more difficult if scholarships are involved. In those cases you need to determine the amount of QE and coordinate that with scholarships. Normally scholarships offset QE and you would take the difference. If some amount of scholarship covered expenses is included in QE you simply need to remember to include that amount in taxable scholarships. Following are a few scenarios to consider.

Simple

If expenses exceed scholarships by more than $4,000, no calculations are necessary. The qualifying expenses are $4,000 and no scholarships are taxable unless they are for non-qualifying expenses.

Elective

If expenses exceed $4,000 and expenses are more than scholarships then you can often take the difference as the initial amount of qualifying expenses. If the initial amount is less than $4,000 and the taxpayer is below the 25% tax bracket you will usually want to include scholarships in income and qualifying expenses until you have $4,000 in qualifying expenses.

If the initial amount is less than $2,000 and the taxpayer is in a tax bracket above 25% then you may only want to include enough to get $2,000 in qualifying expenses. If the initial amount is $2,000 or more and the taxpayer is in a tax bracket above 25% then it will not be beneficial to increase the credit by including scholarships in income. The alignment of the tax brackets and AOTC qualifications are currently such that qualifying single taxpayers will rarely be above the 25% tax bracket, although married filers may be.

Excess Complications

When scholarships exceed expenses then the calculation is a little more advanced. If expenses exceed $4,000, but scholarships are more than expenses, include excess scholarships in income, plus $2,000 of the elective scholarships. If there is still taxable income, include scholarship in income (up to $2,000) to increase the credit until tax is zero.

Family Coordination

One of the quirks you should be aware of when preparing returns with education credits involves coordinating returns of the taxpayer and student. If the taxpayer claims an education credit based on including scholarships in income, it is the student (not the taxpayer) that must include the scholarship in his income. The paid expenses can be moved back and forth, but the scholarships can't. Like many situations when the parent may or may not claim a child, the returns should be coordinated for the most benefit.

One factor to consider is the refundable nature of the credit. If fully nonrefundable, the credit is 100% of the first $2000 and 25% of the next $1000. If the credit is refundable the credit is only 40% of that amount, so the values to consider change. In other words, the refundable credit is 40% of the first $2000 and 10% (40% * 25%) of the next $2000. This 10% is important because if a student must include taxable scholarships in income and it is taxable, the minimum tax rate would be 10%, so the credit is wiped out by that portion of the credit. The student would not want to pay tax on scholarship just to shift that same amount to the parent's credit. If EITC is involved, there may even be a net loss on the claim. Consider the following scenarios.

Parent is claiming the student and the AOTC. Their tax before the credit is $900 and they are in the 15% tax bracket. Qualifying expenses are $6,000. Elective scholarships are $3,500. Net qualifying expenses are then $2,500. Student AGI is $5,500. Parent has the option of claiming on the $2,500 and up to $1500 of the scholarships included in income.

Decision 1: If the parent claims only the $2,500 then their potential credit will be $2,000 + $125 ($500 * 25%) = $2,125. The refundable portion is 40% of that amount ($850) and the nonrefundable portion is limited by their tax ($900). Their total credit is $850 + $900 = $1,750. The student will not owe any tax.

Decision 2: If the parent claims the total $4,000, then the student must include $1500 in income. The potential credit for the parent will then be $2,500. They will receive the refundable amount of $1,000 plus the $900 amount of tax owed for a total of $1,900. Since the student must then add the extra $1,500 to his income, his AGI is now $7,000. The student's taxable bill will then be $80 (($7000 - $6200) * 10%). The net effect is a $1,820 ($1,900 - $80) credit.

Decision 3: If we reduce the taxable scholarships to $700 then the parent's potential credit would be $2,300, composed of the $920 refundable credit and $1,380 nonrefundable credit. The actual credit will be the $920 plus the $900 of tax for a total of $1,820. The student will have income of only $6200, none of which is taxable income.

A different set of circumstances will exist if the tax owed is more than the nonrefundable portion of the credit or the student owes tax before adjustments. To continue this exercise, assume that the parent's tax before the credit is $1,500 and they are in the 15% tax bracket. Qualifying expenses are $6,000. Elective scholarships are $3,500. Net qualifying expenses are then $2,500. Student AGI is $5,500.

Decision 1: If the parent claims only the $2,500 then their potential credit will be $2,000 + $125 ($500 * 25%) = $2,125. The refundable portion is 40% of that amount ($850) and the nonrefundable portion is $1,275. Their total credit is $850 + $1,275 = $2,125. The student will not owe any tax.

Decision 2: If the parent claims the total $4,000, then the student must include $1500 in income. The potential credit for the parent will then be $2,500. They will receive the refundable amount of $1,000 plus the $1,500 amount of tax owed for a total of $2,500. Since the student must then add the extra $1,500 to his income, his AGI is now $7,000. The student's taxable bill will then be $80 (($7000 - $6200) * 10%). The net effect is a $2,420 ($2,500 - $80) credit.

Decision 3: If we reduce the taxable scholarships to $700 then the parent's credit would be $2,300. The student will have income of only $6200, none of which is taxable income.

In this case, Decision 2 provides the highest net benefit.

The best way to proceed may be to prepare the student's return first, allowing the parent to claim on $2000. Then evaluate the taxable income of the student. If below $6,200, add scholarships up to total $6,200. If parent's tax is more than the credit, increase the credit to cover that tax (credit at 40%), and add that amount to the student's taxable income (taxed at 10%). For the second $2,000, if there is no tax on which to use the nonrefundable credit, then re-characterizing the scholarships to claim the refundable credit would be a wash.

Keep in mind that other factors may need to be considered, such as changes in EITC due to AGI. Scholarships are not earned income but the EITC is calculated on both earned income and AGI. The lowest EITC table amount is the amount of the EITC credit. Also, the AOTC credit may be reduced by other credits being claimed on the return.

Avoiding Family Conflict

One of the difficulties in family coordination is that the student may be increasing his taxable income, while the parent is enjoying the credit. In order to avoid family conflict it may be advisable to recommend filing Form 8888 to allocate part of the refund to the student by depositing an amount that offsets the students sacrifice. Alternately the parent could allow the student to do a direct debit from the parent's account for his tax liability due to taxable scholarships. This is not always possible, such as when there is a tax reduction but no refund amount. Ultimately, the taxpayer and student will have to agree on the process before claiming the credit on the student's scholarship inclusion.

Note that the regulations indicate that qualifying expenses can be increased if scholarships are included in income, so scholarship inclusion is a prerequisite. Claiming the credit doesn't require the student to include scholarships in income. Scholarship inclusion is required before the taxpayer can claim the credit. If, however, the student is not required to file a return after consider scholarship inclusion, the taxpayer can assume the amounts have been included in income.

Tax Bracket Watch

When attempting to maximize the credit a good guide is to remember the percentages of each part of the credit. The nonrefundable portion is 100% of the first $2,000, and 25% of the next $2,000. If you are over the 25% tax bracket, then it may be better not include scholarships in income to claim the second $2,000. Similarly the refundable portion amounts to 40% of the first $2,000 and 10% of the second $2,000. For this portion the break-even tax bracket is 10%.

Software Solutions

Now that you understand the law and education credit opportunities, you now need to enter the information into your tax software. This may be one of the hurdles to getting more preparers to consider elective scholarships in education credits.

The following sections review the entries in the more popular packages. Other than TaxWise my observations are based on prior year versions of the software as noted. In some cases, the software will evaluate the credits and deductions and select the most favorable one, but I have yet to review a software package that assists or naturally support scholarship inclusion to maximize education credits. It is up to the preparer to calculate and code the information appropriately.

These are simple examples. If the calculations require using the AOTC Worksheet to determine the amount, use the appropriate amounts from that form. Practically all tax software requires you to enter information for the institution and answer questions related to qualifications for the education credit. If the software does not provide input of scholarships from the 1098T then the expenses entered should be net of those scholarships.

1098T Analysis and Inquiry

Before entering the information it is important to analyze and verify the source documents, particularly the 1098T. Look at the form and ask appropriate questions. When someone comes in with a 1098T the first thing you should do is look at the half-time box. If that is not checked, then that student doesn't qualify for AOTC. But they may qualify for the Lifetime Learning Credit.

Next, see how the expenses are reported on the form. They can report amounts received on amounts billed or amounts actually paid. If box 3 or box 7 is checked, taxpayer will need to provide additional information. If box 7 is checked the amounts shown may include amounts not paid. Even if box 7 is not checked, the amounts may not be accurate if some amounts paid during the tax year were billed in the previous year. If amounts billed for first three months of the next year were actually paid, then the taxpayer can include them in qualifying expenses. Generally scholarships and grants are not paid in advance.

In all cases verify the amounts paid and from what sources. Ask what expenses were paid. Normally all expenses would have been paid if they do not owe the school. Amounts paid by check or through school loans are considered amounts paid. Although I prefer to get account information from school, you can rely on the information provided by the taxpayer. If you don't have account information from the school or a 1098T you should not file for education credits. Claiming education tax credits without proof has been a common method of tax fraud.

Then ask about books and computer expenses that may not be on the 1098T. If they are required expenses they can include them as qualifying expenses paid. You might ask about use of Coverdell ESA, or IRA funds used to pay expenses. This money is tax-free and can cover room and board. Normally you would subtract room and board from this amount (Don't add to qualifying expenses) and subtract the remaining from QE or include in income. A penalty exception applies for IRA distributions. There are many other forms of education benefits.

TaxWise

This is a brief set of instructions for reporting education credits in TaxWise to assist in preparing most returns with AOTC. The process is pretty simple and will be very similar in other tax packages. While TaxWise does require entry of student information and institution information, it doesn't have a 1098T form in the software. In order to explain the calculations, consider the following example:

Example 1: Student has $7,000 in expenses (paid) and scholarships of $5,250 (all from a Pell grant). Box 7 is not checked. He also purchased $720 in books from an on-line retailer.

Preliminary Calculations

Total and enter the information in 8863 including the amount of qualifying expenses. If none of the expenses are paid with scholarships and grants, you can include all expenses on 8863 and you should be finished with preliminaries. If scholarships are reported, you will need to offset expenses with those scholarships. Subtract scholarships from expenses to get initial Qualifying Expenses and enter that amount on 8863. If several items will be included in expenses, you will want to use a scratchpad to identify each one. In this example, $7,000 – $5,250 = $1,750 expenses would initially be entered for qualified education expenses.

	Detail Sheet		2014
Name: BRILLIANT STUDENT		SSN: 123-33-2029	
Description:	EDUCATION CREDIT		
Type			Amount
OUT OF POCKET EXPENSES		▷	1750
			0
			0
			0
			0
			0

Qualified Expenses – Scratch Pad

American Opportunity Credit

27	Adjusted qualified education expenses. See instructions - do not enter more than $4,000	1750
28	Subtract $2,000 from line 27, but not less than -0-	0 ▷
29	Multiply line 28 by 25%	0
30	If line 28 is -0-, amount from line 27. Otherwise, add $2,000 to the amount on line 29. Skip line 31	1750

Qualified Expenses – Form 8863

Entering Other Expenses

If books were not purchased from the institution (AOTC only) add that to qualifying expenses at this point. The initial expenses plus the $720 for books brings the total to $2,470 as reflected on the 8863.

Type	Amount
OUT OF POCKET EXPENSES	1750
BOOKS	720
	0
	0
	0
	0
	0
	0

Qualified Expenses – Books Added

American Opportunity Credit

27	Adjusted qualified education expenses. See instructions - do not enter more than $4,000	2470
28	Subtract $2,000 from line 27, but not less than -0-	470
29	Multiply line 28 by 25%	118▷
30	If line 28 is -0-, amount from line 27. Otherwise, add $2,000 to the amount on line 29. Skip line 31	2118

Qualified Expenses – Updated Form 8863

Scholarship Adjustments

Ask the taxpayer about the nature of the scholarships. If the scholarships include Pell grants, add enough Pell grant money to the expenses in order to bring the total to $4,000. In this case, $4,000 minus the initial $2,470 equals $1,530. We enter that amount first to qualified expenses.

Type	Amount
OUT OF POCKET EXPENSES	1750
BOOKS	720
EXPENSE FROM SCHOLARSHIPS INCLUDED IN INCOME	1530
	0
	0
	0

Qualifed Expenses – Scholarship Adjustment

American Opportunity Credit

27	Adjusted qualified education expenses. See instructions - do not enter more than $4,000	4000
28	Subtract $2,000 from line 27, but not less than -0-	2000▷
29	Multiply line 28 by 25%	500
30	If line 28 is -0-, amount from line 27. Otherwise, add $2,000 to the amount on line 29. Skip line 31	2500

Qualified Expenses – Updated Form 8863

Note: If the amount of the Pell grant is less than the amount calculated, only add that amount to the expenses and adjust the total accordingly.

Adding Scholarship Income

Then you need to add the same amount to Line 7 scholarships. You will need to use the second line on the form and link to a scratch pad. This amount must be identified as scholarships. If it is just included in the Line 7 total, then it would be incorrectly be added to earned income for EITC.

Detail Sheet		2014

Name: BRILLIANT STUDENT   SSN: 123-33-2029

Description: TAXABLE SCHOLARSHIP INCLUDED

Type	Amount
SCHOLARSHIP INCLUDED TO MAXIMIZE EDUCATION CREDIT	1530
	0
	0

Taxable Scholarship – Scratch Pad

Income

7	Wages, salaries, tips, etc.	AB ☐ FB ☐ DCB ☐ SNE ☐ SSHIP ☑	1530
	Taxable scholarship not on Form W2	1530	
	Household employee income not on Form W2	0	
8a	Taxable interest		0
b	Tax-exempt interest	0	
9a	Ordinary dividends including qualified dividends from Forms 8814, listed on Schedule B	0	0
b	Qualified dividends including qualified dividends from Forms 8814, listed on Schedule B	0	

Taxable Scholarship – Form 1040 Line 7

This concludes the calculation of the education credit for this example.

Excess scholarships

Now let's assume that the student has scholarships in excess of expenses. The process is the same except that you initially include the excess scholarships in income instead of including expenses on 8863. The following example illustrates the process in this case.

Example 2: Student has $7,000 in expenses (billed), and $9,000 in scholarships and grants (including a $5,250 Pell grant). She also purchased $720 in books from an on-line retailer.

If scholarships are greater than expenses subtract the expenses from scholarships to get the amount of taxable scholarships. If we assume the student had $9,000 in scholarships and $7,000 in expenses she would include

$2,000 ($9,000 – $7,000) in taxable scholarship income as excess scholarships. Next, she would include any expenses not included on the 1098T such as the $720 in books as qualifying expenses on the 8863. Finally, she would calculate and include enough of the Pell grant in expenses ($4,000 - $720 = $3,280) to maximize AOTC expenses.

However, in this example another issue needs to be addressed. Since there was an excess amount of scholarships, the amount of elective scholarships should be reduced by that amount. The maximizing amount for the credit is $3,280, but the elective amount of the Pell grant is now $5,250 - $2,000 = $3,250 so that limits the amount to add to qualifying expenses and taxable scholarships. The amount $3,250 is now added to both qualifying expenses and taxable scholarships. If using the AOTC worksheet covered elsewhere this issue is resolved automatically. The AOTC worksheet could also be completed and used as the primary input source. The following screenshots show the completed forms for this example.

Type	Amount
BOOKS PURCHASED OUT OF POCKET ▷	720
EXPENSES FROM SCHOLARSHIPS INCLUDED IN INCOME	3250
	0
	0
	0
	0
	0

Qualified Expenses – Scratch Pad

	American Opportunity Credit	
27	Adjusted qualified education expenses. See instructions - do not enter more than $4,000	3970
28	Subtract $2,000 from line 27, but not less than -0-	1970
29	Multiply line 28 by 25%	493
30	If line 28 is -0-, amount from line 27. Otherwise, add $2,000 to the amount on line 29. Skip line 31	2493

Qualified Expenses – Form 8863

Then add the same amount to scholarship income.

Type	Amount
EXCESS SCHOLARSHIPS	2000
SCHOLARSHIPS INCLUDED TO MAXIMIZE EDUCATION CREDIT	3250
	0
	0
	0
	0
	0
	0
	0
	0

Taxable Scholarship – Scratch Pad

Income

7	Wages, salaries, tips, etc.	AB ☐ FB ☐ DCB ☐ SNE ☐ SSHIP ☑					5250
	Taxable scholarship not on Form W2					5250	
	Household employee income not on Form W2					0	
8a	Taxable interest						0
b	Tax-exempt interest					0	
9a	Ordinary dividends including qualified dividends from Forms 8814,						
	listed on Schedule B _____0_____						0

Taxable Scholarship – Form 1040 Line 7

These examples illustrate the treatment of Pell grants. Other scholarships might be able to be treated the same way, but it will require knowing the terms of the scholarship. Note: If scholarships are reported on W-2, report as W-2 earnings. Don't make adjustment to QE or taxable scholarships.

Pro Series (Intuit, 2012)

Pro Series attempts to assist in the calculation of qualifying expenses by providing a 1098T form to enter the amounts being used but it doesn't directly allow you to allocate some scholarships to income. While it attempts to be helpful, it can also be frustrating to find the correct form to enter the information.

Pro Series features a QuickZoom on certain pages that allow the preparer to link to related forms. Because ProSeries 2012 did not list forms in tree form, it becomes more difficult to navigate the forms being used for the Education Credit. Consider the following structure when navigating in Pro Series.

Education Costs (Education Tuition and Fees Summary)

- Student Worksheet(s)
  o 1098T
- 8863

Many boxes also support a supporting statement screen. Note that there may be an 8863 page 2 for each student, but only once 8863 page 1 for the return.

Example 1: Student has 7,000 in expenses (billed) and scholarships of 5,250 (all from a Pell grant). Box 7 is not checked. He purchased 720 in books from an on-line retailer.

Preliminary Entries

Start an education credit in several ways, but the easiest way to find related forms is to start with Education in the Common Forms section.

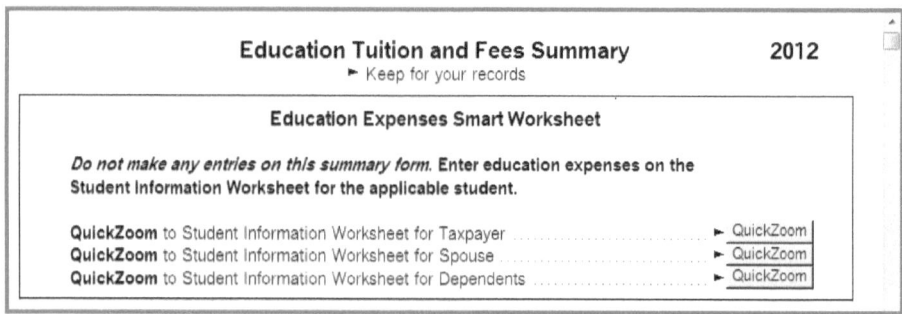

Common Forms - Education

From that sheet, select the appropriate Student Information Worksheet to begin entering the information.

► Keep for your records

Name of Student	Social Security Number
Student Brilliant	123-33-2029

Part I — Student Status

1 Was this person a student during 2012? .... ☒ Yes ☐ No
2 What kind of school did the student attend during 2012? (Check all that apply.)
   a ☐ Elementary   c ☒ College (postsecondary)   e ☐ Military academy
   b ☐ High school (secondary) d ☐ Vocational school   f ☐ Not applicable
   QuickZoom to Form 1098-T Worksheet , Tuition Statement .... ► QuickZoom
   QuickZoom to Form 1099-Q, Payments from Qualified Education Programs .... ► QuickZoom

Student Information Worksheet

After completing the worksheet through Part 3, select QuickZoom to Form 1098T and complete Part I as reported on the 1098T. When possible identify the items (i.e. Pell grants) included in scholarships for future reference.

1098-T Worksheet **Tuition Statement** 2012
► Keep for your records

Taxpayer's name	Social Security No.
Student Brilliant	123-33-2029

1098-T Information (Required):
A A Form 1098-T was received from this institution .... Yes ☒ No ☐
B A Form 1098-T was received from this institution in **2011** with Box 2 filled in and
   Box 7 checked .... Yes ☐ No ☒
Identify Student (Required):
A If student is **Student**
   Check to indicate student .... ► ☒ Taxpayer ☐ Spouse
B If student is
   Double-click to link this 1098-T to the applicable **Dependent Student**
   Information Worksheet .... ►

Filer's name	1 Payments received for qualified
UT Tyler	tuition and related expenses .... $ 7,000.

Street address
3900 Univ Blvd

City	State	Zip Code	2 Amounts billed for qualified tuition
Tyler	TX	75799	and related expenses .... $

Foreign province/county

3 If this box is checked, your educational institution
   has changed its reporting method for 2012 .... ☐

Foreign postal code   Foreign country

Filer's Federal identification number	Student's Social Security Number.	4 Adjustments made for a prior year	5 Scholarships or grants
11-1111111	123-33-2029	$	$ 5,250.

1098T Worksheet

Identify the amounts included in the worksheet by adding a supporting statement.

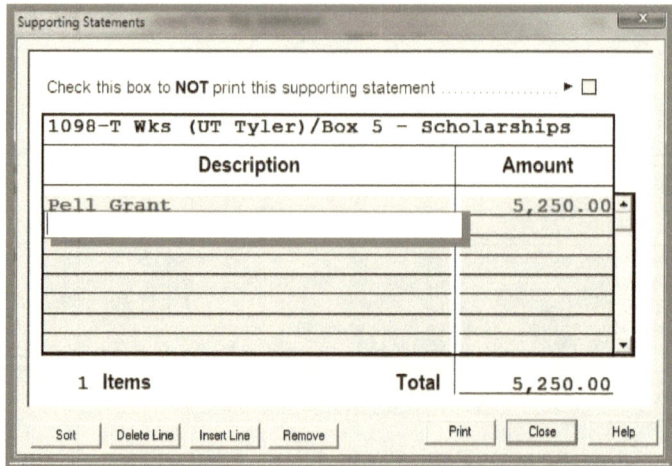

1098T Worksheet – Supporting Statement

Pro Series Help advises that a 1098T form should be completed for all students even if an actual 1098T was not received. This information is linked to the same information required on Form 8863. The bottom of the 1098T form allows you to modify the 1098T amounts for qualifying expenses paid but don't adjust expenses just yet.

Return to Student Information Worksheet and notice that the 1098T information has been included in Part IV. Skip Part V until later.

Part IV – Educational Institution and Tuition Summary

School Name EIN	Address (number, street, apt no., city, state, and ZIP Code)	Tuition paid	Scholarships or grants	On Form 1098-T	Received 2011 1098T with Box 2 filled and box 7 checked?
UT Tyler 11–1111111	3900 Univ Blvd Tyler TX 75799	7,000.	5,250.	Yes ☒ No ☐	Yes ☐ No ☒
If a foreign address: foreign province/state: Postal code: Country:					
				Yes ☐ No ☐	Yes ☐ No ☐
If a foreign address: foreign province/state: Postal code: Country:					
Totals		7,000.	5,250.		

Updated Student Information Worksheet

Entering Other Expenses

Now complete Part VI. This is where books and other expenses not paid to the institution can be entered. The $720 in books has been added to the expenses.

Description	Total	Amount eligible for							
		American Opportunity Credit	Lifetime Learning Credit	Tuition and Fees Deduction	Qualified Higher Education Expense for 529 Plan	Qualified Higher Education Expense for ESA	Qualified Higher Education Expense for US Bonds	Qualified Elementary and Secondary Expense for ESA
		Not Qualified	Not Qualified	Not Qualified	Not Applicable	Not Applicable	Not Applicable	Not Applicable
Expenses:								
1 Tuition paid from Part IV	7,000.	7,000.	7,000.	7,000.				
Paid to institution as a condition of enrollment:								
2 Fees								
3 Books, supplies, equipment								
Paid to other than institution or not a condition of enrollment:								
4 Books, supplies, equipment	720.	720						
5 Other course-related								
6 Room and board								
7 Special needs expenses								
8 Computer expenses								
9 QTP or ESA contribution								
10 Academic tutoring								
11 Uniforms								
12 Transportation								
13 Total qualified expenses	7,720.	7,720.	7,000.	7,000.				

Student Information Worksheet – Additional Expenses

Review the 1098T and reconcile the amounts actually paid if necessary.

Reconciliation of Box 1, Payments Received for Qualified Tuition and Related Expenses

A   Enter box 1 amount **not** paid during 2012 .... 0.
B   Enter box 1 amount actually paid during 2012 .... 7,000.

Reconciliation of Box 2, Amounts Billed for Qualified Tuition and Related Expenses

A   Enter box 2 amount **not** paid during 2012 ....
B   Enter box 2 amount actually paid during 2012 ....

Reconciliation of Box 5, Veteran- or Employer-Provided Assistance Included in Box 5

A   Enter portion of box 5 amount from veteran- or tax free employer-provided assistance .....
B   Enter portion of box 5 amount from employer-provided assistance included in income ......
C   Portion of box 5 amount from scholarships or grants .... 5,250.

Expense Reconciliation

One of the flaws inherent in using a 1098T is that it assumes correct 1098T amounts, and this package doesn't provide any alerts when some of the amounts are for the following year. You may need to change the amount for Box 1 of the 1098T. Use the reconciliation section for Box 1 to show the actual amounts paid.

Scholarship Adjustments

Form 8863, page 2, line 27 should now show the tentative amount of qualifying expenses. Note: This is a total for all students.

If line 27 does not show $4,000 (for one student), consider possible adjustments. In this case Form 8863 shows $2,470. The difference between $2,470 and $4,000 is $1,530. Pell grants are more than $1,530 so we can include that amount in income and increase qualifying expenses.

American Opportunity Credit

27 Adjusted qualified education expenses. **Do not enter more than $4,000**	27	2,470.
28 Subtract $2,000 from line 27. If zero or less enter -0-	28	470.
29 Multiply line 28 by 25% (.25)	29	118.
30 If line 28 is zero, enter the amount from line 27. Otherwise, add $2,000 to the amount on line 29 and enter the result. Skip line 31. Include the total of all amounts from all Part III, line 30 on Part 1, line 1	30	2,118.

Initial Form 8863

Go to Student Information worksheet. Under Scholarships, other, enter -1530. You can use a supporting worksheet to identify that amount.

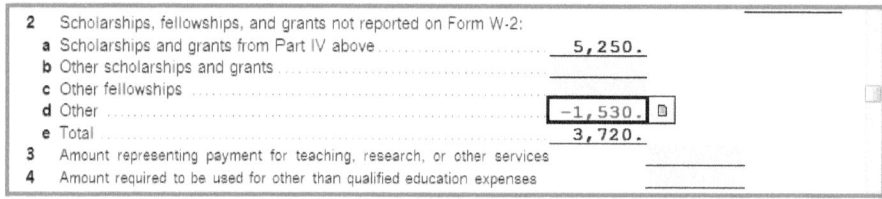

2 Scholarships, fellowships, and grants not reported on Form W-2:		
a Scholarships and grants from Part IV above	5,250.	
b Other scholarships and grants		
c Other fellowships		
d Other	-1,530.	
e Total	3,720.	
3 Amount representing payment for teaching, research, or other services		
4 Amount required to be used for other than qualified education expenses		

Student Information Worksheet – Scholarship Adjustment

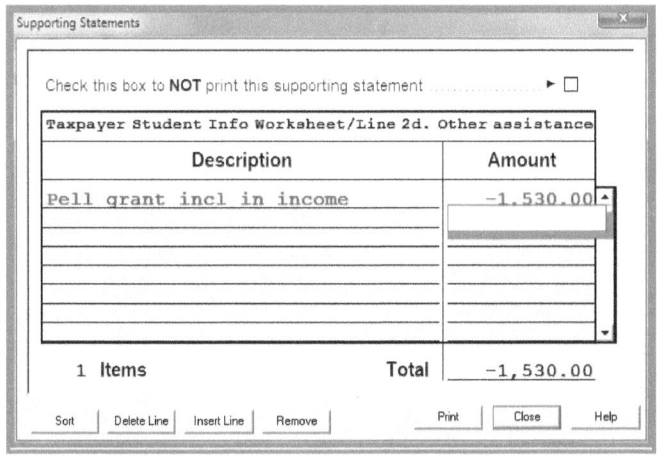

Scholarship Adjustment – Supporting Statement

You will notice that lines 3 and 4 on the Student Information worksheet can be used to enter other types of scholarships. Since there isn't an entry for elective scholarships that the taxpayer elects to include in income, it was necessary to manually adjust scholarship total and manually add the scholarships to income.

Now when you review page 2 of Form 8863, you notice that the credit has been maximized.

American Opportunity Credit

27	Adjusted qualified education expenses. **Do not enter more than $4,000**	27	4,000.
28	Subtract $2,000 from line 27. If zero or less enter -0-	28	2,000.
29	Multiply line 28 by 25% (.25)	29	500.
30	If line 28 is zero, enter the amount from line 27. Otherwise, add $2,000 to the amount on line 29 and enter the result. Skip line 31. Include the total of all amounts from all Part III, line 30 on Part 1, line 1	30	2,500.

Adjusted Form 8863

Adding scholarship income

Now that this amount of scholarships isn't offset by expenses it must be included in income. In the Income section, and under Wage, select Wages, Etc Wks (Wages, Salaries, & Tips Worksheet) and navigate to line 13. This normally does not take a manual entry so you will have to override. Right click and select override or press Ctrl-D. Note that the override will mean the field does not contain scholarship adjustments entered in line 3 or 4, so you should verify all amounts.

9	Other earned income			
10	**Subtotal.** **Add lines 1 through 9**			
11	Taxable employer-provided dependent care benefits, from Form 2441			
12	Taxable employer-provided adoption benefits less any excluded benefits from Form 8839			
13	Scholarship/fellowship income not on Form W-2	1,530.		1,530.
14	Other non-earned income			

Taxable Scholarship

Note: Ideally, the 1098T reconciliation or Student expense worksheet would have a line for this. There are currently only options to enter scholarship wages or scholarships that must be used for non-qualifying expenses. Since Pro Series is not my tax package of choice, more experienced users may have a better method.

Lacerte

Although Lacerte and Pro Series are both from Intuit, they are quite different. The procedure for Lacerte is similar to TaxWise, except that books are entered separately.

Preliminary

Using the same example as in the TaxWise and Pro Series explanations we manually calculate the net amount of qualifying expenses by subtracting tax-free scholarships from total expenses. In this example, $7,000 – $5,250 = $1,750 would be entered. In Lacerte (2013), Select the Credits tax and select Screen 38. For the field identified as qualified tuition and fees click on the box to the right of the input field to access Lacerte notes, enter the amount, and identify as Out Of Pocket expenses. These notes are the same as Detail Sheets in TaxWise and the Supporting Statements in Pro Series.

Current Year Expenses

NOTE: Enter education expenses below not entered elsewhere.

Blank=optimize, 1=force credit, 2=force tuition deduction . . . .

Qualified tuition and fees (net of nontaxable benefits)   1,750

Books and supplies required to be purchased from the institution . . . .

Books and supplies not entered above (AOC only)

Qualified Expenses - Initial

Supporting Detail

Title
Education Credits / Tuition Deduction
Qualified tuition and fees (net of nontaxable benefits)

Print as
⦿ Don't print   ○ Worksheet   ○ Statement

☐ Proforma descriptions

Description	Amount
Out of Pocket Expenses	1,750

Total   1,750

Qualified Expenses - Note

71

The section head of Current Year Expenses can be misleading. It suggests that the expenses are limited to the current year. Remember that the taxpayer can pay qualifying expenses in advance for the first three months of the following year.

Entering Other Expenses

Lacerte has two separate fields for entering books. The first field is for books required to be purchased from the institution. The second field is for all other books. Entries in the second field will not be qualifying expenses for the Lifetime Learning Credit. Enter the amount in the appropriate field.

Current Year Expenses	
NOTE: Enter education expenses below not entered elsewhere.	
Blank=optimize, 1=force credit, 2=force tuition deduction	
Qualified tuition and fees (net of nontaxable benefits)	1,750
Books and supplies required to be purchased from the institution	
Books and supplies not entered above (AOC only)	720

Qualified Expenses – Books Added

Scholarship Adjustments

Form 8863, page 2, line 27 should now show the tentative amount of qualifying expenses. If line 27 does not show $4,000 (for one student), consider possible adjustments. In this case Form 8863 shows $2,470. The difference between $2,470 and $4,000 is $1,530. Pell grants are more than $1,530 so we can include that amount in income and increase qualifying expenses.

	American Opportunity Credit		
27	Adjusted qualified education expenses (see instructions). Do not enter more than $4,000	27	2,470.
28	Subtract $2,000 from line 27. If zero or less enter -0-.	28	470.
29	Multiply line 28 by 25% (.25).	29	118.
30	If line 28 is zero, enter the amount from line 27. Otherwise, add $2,000 to the amount on line 29 and enter the result. Skip line 31. Include the total of all amounts from all Parts III, line 30 on Part I, line 1.	30	2,118.
	Lifetime Learning Credit		
31	Adjusted qualified education expenses (see instructions). Include the total of all amounts from all Parts III, line 31, on Part II, line 10	31	
BAA	FDIA3602L 12/26/13		Form 8863 (2013)

Form 8863

Add $1,530 for expenses and identify as Scholarships included in Income. This will bring the total of qualified tuition and fees to $3,280.

Current Year Expenses

NOTE: Enter education expenses below not entered elsewhere.

Blank=optimize, 1=force credit, 2=force tuition deduction	
Qualified tuition and fees (net of nontaxable benefits)	3,280
Books and supplies required to be purchased from the institution	
Books and supplies not entered above (AOC only)	720

Qualified Expenses – Scholarships Added

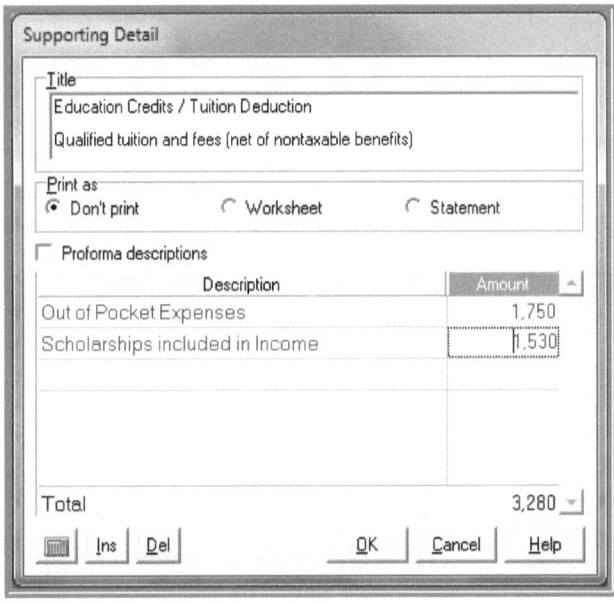

Supporting Detail

Title

Education Credits / Tuition Deduction

Qualified tuition and fees (net of nontaxable benefits)

Print as
- (•) Don't print   ( ) Worksheet   ( ) Statement

[ ] Proforma descriptions

Description	Amount
Out of Pocket Expenses	1,750
Scholarships included in Income	1,530

Total   3,280

Ins   Del   OK   Cancel   Help

Qualified Expenses – Notes Adjusted

The 8863 should now show \$4,000 on line 27 for qualified education expenses and calculate the potential amount of credit as \$2,500.

American Opportunity Credit

27	Adjusted qualified education expenses (see instructions). Do not enter more than \$4,000	27	4,000.
28	Subtract \$2,000 from line 27. If zero or less enter -0-	28	2,000.
29	Multiply line 28 by 25% (.25)	29	500.
30	If line 28 is zero, enter the amount from line 27. Otherwise, add \$2,000 to the amount on line 29 and enter the result. Skip line 31. Include the total of all amounts from all Parts III, line 30 on Part I, line 1.	30	2,500.

Lifetime Learning Credit

31	Adjusted qualified education expenses (see instructions). Include the total of all amounts from all Parts III, line 31, on Part II, line 10	31	

BAA	FDIA3602L 12/26/13	Form **8863** (2013)

Form 8863 - Adjusted

Adding Scholarship Income

Now that this amount of scholarships isn't offset by expenses it must be included in income. In Lacerte that entry is made in Screen 14.1, Miscellaneous in the Alimony and Other Income section. Identify the amount in the note as Scholarships to Increase Education Expenses.

Social Security Benefits Frequently Asked Questions				
	Taxpayer	Spouse	Prior Year TP	Prior Year SP
Social security benefits (SSA-1099, box 5)				
Medicare premiums paid (SSA-1099)				
1=treat Medicare premiums paid as SE health insurance				
Tier 1 railroad retirement benefits (RRB-1099, box 5)				
Taxable social security & railroad retirement [O]				
1=lump-sum election for social security benefits				
Alimony and Other Income				
Alimony received				
Excess salary deferrals				
Taxable scholarships and fellowships	1,530			
Jury duty pay				
Household employee income not on W-2				

Taxable Scholarships Added to Income

Supporting Detail

Title

Miscellaneous Income

Taxable scholarships and fellowships

Print as
- ⦿ Don't print
- ○ Worksheet
- ○ Statement

☐ Proforma descriptions

Description	Amount
Scholarships to Increase Education Expenses	1,530

Total	1,530

[Ins] [Del]   [OK] [Cancel] [Help]

Taxable Scholarships Added - Notes

Drake (2013)

Education Credits in Drake are handled the same way as TaxWise and Lacerte, by manually calculating and entering the net amount of expenses and the amount of taxable scholarships. Double-clicking on the field allows you to attach a Detail worksheet to the input as in the former programs.

ATX (2012)

Education Credits in ATX is mostly manual as well, although the input screens for Form 8863 does have a line for American Opportunity Credit course materials. It does not provide input for scholarships though so expenses should be entered net of scholarships. ATX also does not have a calculating Detail sheet. The notes that can be added to a field are text based only.

TaxSlayer (2013)

TaxSlayer will also require the preparer to make all calculations manually without the benefit of a worksheet or detail sheet.

Others

It is crucial that the preparer knows how to calculate the relevant amounts for education credits. They will only need to know the software they are using, but it is to their advantage to understand all of the details. At a minimum, the preparer should prepare sample returns using the examples providing in Publication 17, and Treas. Reg. § 1.25A-5.

Documentation of the required procedures, similar to the examples in this text, will go a long way toward eliminating confusion during tax season.

Planning

Timing Techniques

Education credits have particular requirements that make timing an important part of claiming those credits. Taxpayers may be limited to a certain amount each year, and a limited number of years. The amount of the taxpayer's taxable income and tax owed will be another important factor. Dependency and other factors could also play a role in the planning process.

Half-time At Least One Semester

The credit does require a student to be at least half-time at least one semester in the tax year, but once that requirement is met all qualifying expenses can be used. If a student attends the first semester and then takes a single class in each of the following semesters, all expenses can be used. They also have the option of prepaying for a class at the beginning of the following tax year (IRC § 25A(b)(2)(B)).

While it is conventional to speak of credits in terms of semesters some institutions operate on a quarter system. Semesters are important because they generally cover at least one day in each of 5 months and can determine if the student is a full-time student for dependency reasons. The code for education credits does not include that limitation, only indicating that the student must be half-time during at least one academic period. Academic period is defined in Treas. Reg. § 1.25A-2(c) as "a quarter, semester, trimester, or other period of study as reasonably determined by an eligible educational institution." In cases where the credit is being claimed for a dependent, the student may need to be full-time for two quarters in order to meet the 5-month requirement included in IRC § 152(f)(2).

Prepayments

One method to accelerate qualifying expenses is to make allowable prepayments. To maximize the potential benefits it may be possible due to Treas. Reg. § 1.25A-5(e)(2) to pay for the final semester in the prior year. Prepayments must apply to expenses incurred in the first three months of the subsequent year. You do not have to pay all of the tuition, and you could purchase some of the books in advance. This is a case where the preparer should be familiar with the client's family situation. If a child will be graduating in the following year, question them about the possibility of making prepayments to maximize the AOTC. This could also be beneficial if the student is receiving their undergraduate degree in December.

Graduate School Expenses

It is also possible that the AOTC can be used to pay for the first two semesters of graduate school. If a student graduates in May and then attends graduate school through the end of the year (summer and fall), all expenses for the year qualify for the AOTC. It may be better to forego the claim on the student's first school year so that they have the opportunity to claim the AOTC for this year. Form 8863 instructions are correct in indicating that the student cannot have earned a degree before the **start of the tax year**. Comments added to the final Treas. Reg. § 1.25A-3(d)(2) clarify that qualified expenses paid during the entire taxable year may be included in calculating the credit even if the student had completed their (then) first two years of undergraduate study during the year. Understanding the benefits to graduate students can be important since other benefits, such as the Pell grant, go away at the same time tuition costs increase.

Four Choice Years

Typically, school years span five taxable years, with the student only going to school one semester in each of the first and last years, but the AOTC can only be claimed for four years. If the student has limited expenses in some semesters she may wish to wait until years where qualifying expenses are greater, or a final semester when she has taxable income where she can take advantage of the nonrefundable portion of the AOTC.

In one common scenario the credit can be claimed for each of the first four tax years with the final tax year paid in advance. In another scenario the taxpayer could forego the credit in the first tax year (one semester), and claim the credit in the other four years with some graduate level expenses included in the year of graduation.

Change of Plans

If necessary, it may be to the benefit of the taxpayer to amend tax returns to maximize the total benefit. Since some years can be amended it may be possible to make some adjustments there but years outside of the statue of limitations should be evaluated carefully. For example, since amendments are limited to the past three years, the taxpayer may not want to waste the initial AOTC year on a smaller amount of credit.

Expiration Date

Don't forget the expiration date. With the current law scheduled to expire in 2017, and no surety that it will be extended, few years remain to allow for planning how and when to use education credits.

Coordinating with other benefits

Just as important as understanding the elective nature of traditional scholarships, federal grants, and AOTC qualified expenses, practitioners should be aware of how they potentially interact with educational costs such as room and board or computer technology. Whenever possible, practitioners should look for the best combination of benefits and work to coordinate them. This is particularly true if other sources are involved.

This information on other benefits is general in nature so taxpayers will need to do additional research and/or consult a personal financial planner before making plans with these instruments. Several benefits that can be used with education credits are retirement or savings related. Two are specifically for education while traditional or Roth IRAs could also be used for educational expenses. With the exception of traditional IRAs, each benefit discussed is after-tax, so that the contributions to these plans are not deductible. Additionally, if the benefit is not used for educational expenses the taxpayer may be subject to tax and/or penalties on distributions. Possible changes in these plans have also been in the news, so it would be wise to review current regulations on a regular basis.

Section 529 & Coverdell

Section 529 and Coverdell Educational Savings Accounts are two savings options for education. The programs have distinct differences but they do work together and have many similarities. The code in Section 530 often refers to descriptions and restrictions included in Section 529 or vice versa.

Section 529 provides tax exempt status to qualified tuition programs as defined in IRC § 529(b), including programs which provide tuition credits, or which accepts contributions to pay for qualified higher education expenses (QHEE) of the beneficiary. Programs are generally established by a state agency or educational institution.

Next to the Section 529 program is the Coverdell ESA in Section 530. A Coverdell is a trust created for the purpose of paying qualified educational expenses for a designated beneficiary. There is also a $2,000 annual contribution limit for the Coverdell and contributions cannot be made after the beneficiary is age 18. One characteristic of the Coverdell ESA is that distributions can also be used for elementary and secondary education expenses but all amounts must be distributed by the time the beneficiary is age 30. It is possible, though, to convert the trust to a new account or beneficiary.

In both Section 529 plans and Coverdell accounts contributions are not deductible but distributions are tax free if used for qualifying educational expenses. Although not deductible, lower-income taxpayers may be able to avoid taxation if their taxable income is lower. Distributions in both plans can be considered elective scholarships in the calculation of education credits.

These plans are also important because some expenses allowed are not qualifying expenses for education credits. Specifically, the terms in IRC § 529(e)(3)(B)(i) allow amounts withdrawn to pay for room and board expenses for students attending at least half-time. Thus, even though housing costs paid from a Coverdell or Section 529 can be tax-free; those amounts do not offset qualified expenses includable for the purpose of education credits. Publication 970 also confirms this by describing how to coordinate with other aid to maximize education credits.

Penalties

The inclusion of an amount from these plans in income may be subject to a 10% penalty. Distributions, however, are not subject to a penalty provided the student receives a qualified scholarship that is used for qualifying expenses or uses the amount to claim an education credit. A qualified scholarship is that portion of a scholarship used to pay qualified education expenses. The exclusion based on receipt of a scholarship applies only to the extent the distribution is not more than the scholarship, allowance, or payment (IRC §§ 530(d)(4)(B)(iii) and (2)(C)(i)(II)).

Additionally, the penalty does not apply if the distribution is included in income only because the qualified education expenses were taken into account in determining the American opportunity or lifetime learning credit (IRC § 530(d)(4)(B)(v)). The same rule applies to Section 529 distributions (IRC § 529(c)(6)). Form 1099-Q issued to the beneficiary provides the amount of the distribution, basis, and earnings on which to calculate tax liability. Form 5329 is used to report any taxable earnings or penalty.

Computers

One bonus of Coverdell is that certain computer technology purchases are now included in the list of **elementary** and **secondary** expenses that can be paid for by a qualified tuition program. The definition of qualified expenses in Section 530(e)(3)(A)(iii) includes computer technology, equipment, and Internet access if they are used by the beneficiary and family. Carefully note that the computer expense for family and beneficiary was a qualified **higher education** expense for 2009 or 2010 only, according to Section 529(e)(3)(A)(iii).

Otherwise, computer equipment is only a qualified expense for purposes of the AOTC if it is required.

Q7. Does an expenditure for a computer qualify for the American opportunity tax credit?

A. Whether an expenditure for a computer qualifies for the credit depends on the facts. An expenditure for a computer would qualify for the credit if the computer is needed as a condition of enrollment or attendance at the educational institution.[7]

IRAs

IRAs are treated similar to Section 529 and Coverdell savings accounts in relation to taxability of earnings and penalties if distributed and used for non-qualified educational expenses. Though not specifically an educational account, currently amounts in an Individual Retirement Account (IRA) can be withdrawn and used for educational purposes without penalty (IRC § 72(t)(2)(E)). Traditional IRAs are pre-tax dollars that must be included in income when distributed. If distributed prior to retirement for certain needs, including qualifying educational expenses, they also avoid early distribution penalties. Roth IRAs are after-tax and distributions from contributions are not taxed. Earnings are taxable if withdrawn before age 59½ but are not subject to a 10% early withdrawal penalty if used for qualified educational expenses. Roth IRAs also require that contributions were held for at least 5 years (IRC § 408A(d)(3)(F)(i)(II) and Treas. Reg. 1.408A-6(b)).

Choosing between IRA and educational savings

If you must choose between a Section 529 and an IRA, an IRA may be the more versatile. Consider an educational account after making the maximum amount of IRA contributions. Unlike IRAs, contributions to a 529 or Coverdell, are locked in and can only be used for educational expenses. Also payments from a Roth IRA will generally not be considered as income, whereas Section 529 accounts may affect income for financial aid determination. The interaction of these accounts and financial aid should be investigated carefully.

IRAs have the added benefit of qualifying for the current Retirement Savings Credit when contributions are made and distributions are not required when the beneficiary is a certain age. A Coverdell ESA is designed

---

[7] http://www.irs.gov/uac/American-Opportunity-Tax-Credit:-Questions-and-Answers, Accessed 3/25/2014.

for saving for a beneficiary under age 18 so you can't use it to save for your own education. An IRA, however, can be treated like an education IRA for any family member. Like the Coverdell, qualified expenses for the IRA include room and board for students that are at least half-time. One other benefit of an IRA is the ability to manage the account and invest the funds any way you want. After you have set up a Section 529 plan, neither the contributor or a beneficiary is allowed to direct the investments in the program (IRC § 529 (b)(4)).

There are some ways in which Section 529 accounts are better. For one, minimum contributions to start a 529 are generally lower than that of an IRA. Many fund companies require $2,500 per year to start an IRA (although the myRA will be an option when it becomes available). Before making a plan, make a thorough analysis of the benefits, risks, and potential for each person's circumstances and the available resources at the time. It's also possible that distributions could occur at a time that the taxpayer does not have any taxable consequences.

Strategy

A primary strategy for the use of IRA and educational savings in paying education and claiming education credits would be to use amounts from tax-free aid (Section 529, Coverdell, etc.) to cover room and board, which qualify as tax-free under those code sections; and if needed, use other scholarships as income to increase qualified expenses for the purposes of the education credits.

These are only a couple of things to consider when coordinating benefits. There are many other rules related to these accounts and it would be wise to examine all of the consequences, including their affect on financial aid qualifications. There are a number of books on Section 529 plans and taxpayers may also want to consult a personal financial planner if they are considering using savings plans to fund a significant amount of their education expenses.

Other tax benefits

Education Credits are just one source of funding for education and taxpayers should consider other benefits if they do not qualify for the credits. Since you generally cannot mix benefits for the same child a decision must be made based on which is most beneficial for each child. Since AOTC is the most generous and a portion of it is refundable, consider that before looking at other tax benefits.

The other two most common tax benefits are the Lifetime Learning Credit and the Tuition Deduction. Qualifying expenses include books only if purchased from the institution. Although qualified expenses do not include nonacademic fees such as student activity fees, according to IRC § 25A(f)(1)(C)), they are included if they are required as a condition of enrollment (Treas. Reg. § 1.25A-2(d)(2)(iii)). Some academic fees are never included, including transportation expenses such as parking fees (Treas. Reg. § 1.25A(d)(3)). The limit on LLC is $2,000 per return, while the AOTC is limited on a per-student basis. Like AOTC, taxpayers have the option of including scholarships in income to increase the credit. As mentioned previously, consider the overall effect.

The tuition deduction reduces the amount of tax by changing the amount of taxable income. As a deduction the benefit to a particular taxpayer is reflected in their marginal tax rate. Generally speaking, if the taxpayer is in a tax bracket higher than 20% (LLC credit amount) the tuition deduction will be the best choice. The rules for LLC and the tuition deduction are different so it will be necessary to determine if the taxpayer qualifies before making that decision. Finally, because the tuition deduction is a reduction of AGI it could interact with AOTC for another student and any other item linked to the AGI. Modifications of AGI for the AOTC don't include adjustments for the tuition deduction.

The Education Savings Bond Program is another option for educational savings and can apply to undergraduate and graduate coursework. This program can be used in conjunction with Coverdell and Section 529 qualified tuition programs. Properly used, interest is excluded from taxable income. Employer-Provided Educational Assistance is yet another avenue for financing educational expenses tax-free.

Amending

Amending for Education Credits

When practitioners see clients they often like to see the prior year's return(s). That helps them to know what kind of credits and deductions they have taken in the past, or highlights a carryover for the current tax year. A bright preparer will also reverse that logic. If he discovers that the taxpayer has credits or deductions this year that were not reported on the prior year's return he can question the taxpayer about whether he qualified for credits and deductions for the prior year, and then amend those returns. At that time, they may want to review the other two prior returns as well.

Many taxpayers may be left in the dark because institutions are not required to prepare 1098-Ts when all expenses are paid for by scholarships and grants. Practitioners should question any taxpayer in school, or with children in school about the nature of their educational expenses. Locally I would advise asking about credits claimed for going to a college that limits when they provide a 1098T.

If taking advantage of Regulation 1.25A-5 in maximizing education credits is a new revelation, amending prior year returns can multiply the benefit by a factor of four and potentially earn $10,000 in education credits. The net amount may be less if scholarships are included in income since only 40% of the credit is refundable. When filing a return in the spring semester of the student's senior year a taxpayer (student or parent) can amend returns for his freshman, sophomore, and junior year at the same time he files his senior year return. As previously mentioned, there may be years that are more beneficial than others, so planning is still a factor.

Amending returns could also be used to change prior year decisions related to education credits. If you didn't maximize the credit in one year and you can in a following year, you may want to amend. You need to be careful, however, since you could be subject to late payment penalties if you have to repay for the credit.

You can amend tax returns up to 3 years after their due date (without extensions). Thus, tax years 2011, 2012, and 2013 can all be amended before April 15 of 2015. If you do not have copies of your return, you can access your tax return information from the IRS website.

IRS transcript

The IRS makes taxpayers prior year return information available on line using transcripts. The actual return is not there but the information you will need to review or amend a return is available. Using your browser go to

http://www.irs.gov/Individuals/Get-Transcript

irs.gov – Get Transcript

Select Get Transcript Online

Get Transcript - Login

Log in to the site with your User ID and password (next screen). If you have not logged in before you will have to create an account. The IRS will ask several questions to verify your identity.

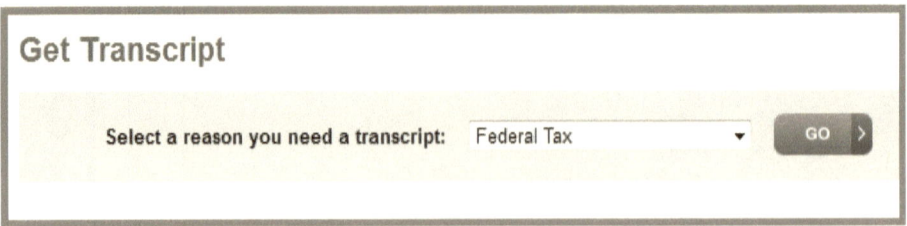

Select a reason for requesting your transcript: **Federal Tax**

You selected: Federal Tax
We suggest you download: Record of Account Transcript

Below are the transcripts and years available.

Return Transcript

2013
2012
2011
2010

Record of Account Transcript

2013
2012
2011
2010

Glossary

Return Transcript
Tax Return Transcripts show most line items from your tax return (Form 1040, 1040A or 1040EZ) as it was originally filed, including any accompanying forms and schedules. This transcript does not reflect any changes you, your representative or the IRS made after you filed your return. In many cases, a Return Transcript will meet the requirements of lending institutions offering mortgages and student loans.

Account Transcript

2013	2012	2011
2010	2009	N/A
N/A	N/A	N/A
N/A		

Wage & Income Transcript

2013	2012	2011
2010	2009	2008
2007	2006	2005
2004		

Record of Account Transcript
Record of Account Transcripts combine the information from tax account and tax return transcripts.

Account Transcript

Show Less ▭   Show Less ▭

Federal Tax Transcripts

Record of Account Transcript (includes return transcript) for year

Select the tax year you want to retrieve. The tax year is the year before you file your return. Choose **Save File** and name the file with the tax year, like *2013TaxTranscript.pdf.* While you are there, you may want to get all four years available. Print or provide the files to your preparer.

Explaining the American Opportunity Tax Credit

When I talk to a taxpayer about their return and the potential of claiming the American Opportunity Tax Credit (AOTC), they often are confused about it, especially if the AOTC involves including scholarships in income. I've struggled with how to explain it and continually expand or contract the explanation depending on how much I think they understand. In cases where the student and parent must coordinate their returns to get the biggest credit the explanation is even more critical since it must be relayed to the other person.

This is my effort to outline the basics of the AOTC in an orderly and progressive way. The actual rules are more complex but this should help taxpayers understand what is happening. The first 5 include the basics. The second half deals with scholarships mixed in.

1	The American Opportunity Tax Credit (AOTC) is available for the first $4,000 of qualifying educational expenses. The credit amount is calculated at 100% of the first $2,000 and 25% of the next $2,000.
2	Only 40% of the credit is refundable (max $1,000), and there are separate qualifying rules for the refundable part. The rest of it can only reduce the amount of tax paid.
3	Amounts paid in cash, credit, loans, or by third-parties are included in qualifying expenses. The amounts may be reported on a 1098T but the taxpayer may need to verify the amounts with the student's financial account. A 1098T is not required.
4	Qualifying expenses are amounts paid for tuition, books, and related expenses. Other expenses such as room and board don't count as qualifying expenses.
5	The AOTC is claimed on the return for which the student is being claimed as a dependent. If the student is claimed as a dependent on someone else's return the student cannot claim the AOTC.
6	If you receive scholarships that cover some of your expenses, they reduce the total amount of qualifying expenses. *Example 1: If you have qualifying expenses of $3,000 and scholarships of $2,000, the net amount of qualifying expenses available for claiming the AOTC is $1,000.*
7	If scholarships are more than expenses, include the excess in income. *Example 2: If you have qualifying expenses of $3,000 and scholarships of $4,000, the amount of qualifying expenses is $0, and you have to include the additional $1,000 scholarship amount in income.*
8	Some (not all!) scholarships can be included in income to increase your qualifying expenses. Pell grants can be treated that way. *Using example 1, if you have qualifying expenses of $3,000 and the $2,000 scholarship is a Pell grant you can include all of the scholarship in income and claim an AOTC on the full $3,000.* *Using example 2, if you have qualifying expenses of $3,000 and the $4,000 scholarship is a Pell grant you have to include all $4,000 of the scholarship in income to claim the AOTC on the $3,000 expenses.*
9	Scholarships are always the responsibility of the student. In order for the person claiming the dependency exemption (i.e. parent) to claim the maximum AOTC, the **student** may have to include scholarships in their income. *Using example 1 again, if the student includes the $2,000 in income, the parent can then claim the credit on all $3,000 in expenses. If the student is at the 10% tax bracket, it will cost $200, but the parent can reduce their tax by up to $2,250. If they don't owe tax to reduce they may still get $900.*
10	Including scholarships in income doesn't always mean you have to pay tax on it. If your deductions and exemptions are more than your income, you won't have to pay income tax.

Special Issues

The reporting for Education Credits could affect a number of other areas, so a careful eye is essential. These are just a few possible side effects or concerns to watch out for.

AGI

By including scholarships in income AGI increases and tax may be owed on the scholarship amounts. The first $2,000 of expenses generates a 100% tax credit, but the second $2,000 only generates a 25% tax credit. If the marginal tax rate is above 25%, then it may be better to only include $2,000 of elective scholarships in income. The increase in AGI could also initiate phase-outs or subject the taxpayer to AMT.

AOTC Phase-out:

AOTC is subject to a phase-out. The phase-out is essentially based on percentage of income between lower and upper phase-out limits. Thus, $1000 over (based on $10,000 range) would reduce your credit by 10%.

If you happen to be put into the phase-out range by including scholarships and grants in income, re-calculate the credit omitting some or all of the scholarships to determine the most advantageous treatment. Generally, it will be most advantageous to include the first $2000 of expenses regardless of including scholarships in income. Above the first $2000, the net benefit will largely depend on your marginal tax rate and deductions.

Credit Offsets

The AOTC may be offset by other nonrefundable credits. If the total of the nonrefundable credits is more than the tax before scholarship adjustments, the taxpayer may not benefit from attempting to increase the credit. Ideally, only make adjustments up to the point that tax liability is reduced to zero. Evaluate the benefits on a case-by-case basis.

Earned Income

One of the characteristics of taxable scholarships is that it is not earned income for purposes of the EITC. Scholarship income is excluded from earned income in the calculation of the earned income credit, so be sure to report and treat it that way. Include SCH and the amount to the left of line 7 on 1040. Failing to tag that income in the margin as SCH could lead the IRS to believe you understated income. The IRS may make corrections to EITC and send the taxpayer an additional earned income credit which he doesn't deserve, and may have to repay. Only amounts you receive for teaching, research, or other services would be considered earned income. Those amounts are not tax-free scholarships although they can be used to pay education expenses qualifying for education credits.

Changes in EITC

Although scholarships are not earned income for EITC, they can affect it negatively. EITC is initially calculated on earned income in the EITC worksheet, but it is then calculated based on AGI. The lower credit amount is what the taxpayer receives. The net benefit of including the scholarships should always be considered. This is particularly true if claiming the Lifetime Learning Credit. In your software, you may be able to incrementally include scholarship income to determine at what point the income reduces the net benefit. Then you can use that amount to calculate the credit.

Support

Scholarships as support should not be a concern with current laws. If scholarships are used for qualified education expenses, they are not considered support in determining dependency (IRC §§ 152(c)(1)(D) and (f)(5)). The code here does not define the nature of the scholarships not treated as support. Also of concern in evaluating support is the fact that the refundable portion of the education credit may require the taxpayer to provide over half of their support with earned income. Refer to the qualifications flowchart for the order of qualifications.

Education Credit Fraud

The benefits associated with education credits have recently been a target of tax fraud. At one point the IRS was holding and examining returns with education credits more closely. In 2013, many of the problems associated with education credits were due to forms not being completed properly, either through preparer negligence or software error. Then, earlier this year the Treasury Inspector General for Tax Administration released a report claiming that billions are paid for potentially erroneous education credit claims. Some issues involve claiming AOTC for more than four years, claiming for students that are not half-time, and claiming for expenses that are not at an eligible educational institution.

None of the fraud has reportedly been related to options made available in Regulation 1.25A-5 or the elective treatment of scholarships. Instead, the cases that made their way to Tax Court had more to do with the plain language of basic qualifications such as age requirements, dependency exemptions, actual expenses[8], prepayments[9], and phase-outs.

The only case I found that concerned Treas. Reg. § 1.25A-5 was a discussion of the change in a Louisiana program (TOPS) previously mentioned. Incidentally, the fact that there are so few cases that deal with the elective nature of scholarship income suggests that these regulations may be underutilized.

The TIGTA report may not be that dismal since it identified most of the credits as potentially erroneous simply because a 1098T was not provided. A 1098T is not required and the report does not indicate that they are aware of that. That presumption highlights one of the biggest flaws of education credit laws. Without a 1098T the IRS does not know if a student is half-time, or if even attending. Even with a 1098T, the IRS has no way to determine whether a credit is fraudulent without knowing all costs, payments, and options available to the taxpayer. That would require institutions to not only issue 1098Ts for all students, but also report scholarships and grants and their treatment options, and that would only provide them with the information needed to investigate returns. The limited 1098T reporting requirements are allowed by Treasury regulations (Treas. Reg. § 1.6050S-1(a)(2)(iii)) and not in the law (IRC § 6050S), and it appears that Congress is not willing to demand more complete reporting.

Still, the TIGTA is pressuring the IRS to lower the fraud rate for education credits, so it is imperative that taxpayers have and retain documentation to support their education credit claims. See the section on Documentation below.

Common Education Credit Errors

The IRS has a list of the most common education credit errors at http://www.eitc.irs.gov/Other-Refundable-Credits/aotcllc/errors. The following summarizes the most common mistakes taxpayers make for which a claim may be denied.

- A student that did not attend a college, university or vocational school
- Eligible education expenses were not paid or not considered as paid
- Expenses were unqualified expenses
- Credit for an eligible student for more than 4 years

---

[8] Adams v Comm'r, Tax Court Summary Opinion 2013-57.
[9] Jayesh B. v Comm'r, Tax Court Summary Opinion 2006-40.

- Deduction for Tuition and Fees on Form 1040, line 34 was made for the same student.

Although preparers will usually know the limitations of the AOTC, the taxpayer may not. A thorough review of the client or familiarity with the client's situation is essential to avoid these pitfalls. These are only the most common errors. Preparers should review all qualifications for each claim for the credit.

1098-T

Although the 1098-T may not be accurate or required to claim an education credit, the IRS may look at their 1098-T records to determine if a student was attending a college or university. Colleges and universities are not required to submit or provide a 1098-T to their students in many cases. If one is not on file, the taxpayer could receive a Form 886-H-AOC requesting alternate proof of attendance. The form details the information that the IRS is requesting. This is where documentation is important.

Documentation

Keep all documents that may be requested by the IRS. The taxpayer may need to provide documentation for education credits to show qualifying expenses paid, student qualifications, or information about the education program. Required documentation will be different depending on the credit or deduction claimed and the taxpayer's individual circumstances.

Receipts

Receipts for expenses are necessary to prove expenses. The student's school account records can provide much of this support. The list of expenses provided on the school account information should be detailed enough to show which expenses are qualifying expenses for the particular credit. Receipts for books purchased elsewhere will also need to be kept.

Course Descriptions and Degree Plan

Additional requirements may include a description of the courses, including what books are required for the courses, and the degree plan. Optional books are not considered qualifying expenses although they may be listed on the course syllabus along with required books for the course. Although the course syllabus typically outlines the required books, individual instructors may require different texts. That should be documented at the time. Emails or other documents from the instructor may be useful in this case.

Scholarship Terms

If the credit was increased by including scholarships and grants in income it may be necessary to document scholarship inclusion support. Just as you would document that amounts were paid, or that a scholarship was used for qualified expenses, you should document your ability to treat scholarships as taxable income. Keep some official source document that says the scholarship may be used for other than qualified expenses, i.e. room and board. Official letters from the institution or printouts from official web pages would be some examples.

Family Coordination

If scholarships were included in the income of the student to increase the parent's credit amount, that information should be maintained. This should be done even though a student's scholarship income doesn't require the student to file a tax return.

Questions

There are some questions related to education credits. Here's a few I've come up with.

Books purchased by a third party (not at institution)

The regulations say that an amount paid to the institution is considered an amount paid by the taxpayer. The taxpayer can also include expenses paid for required books and supplies even though they are not paid to the institution. But, what about amounts paid by a third party for required books purchased outside of the institution? Are those also considered paid by the taxpayer? Since the law does not specifically include that in the description, the taxpayer should assume that they do not, although IRS publications do not list that as a restriction.

Regulation Example Confusion

One of the areas where the law is unclear concerning AOTC is the wording of examples in the regulations that appear to conflict with the procedures for determining qualified expenses for the credit. Given the examples some have argued that the taxpayer must have paid expenses out of pocket, or that the taxpayer must have had non-qualifying expenses. While my opinion is that examples within the regulations are like Private Letter Rulings, in that they cover specific scenarios and do not have the power to alter the primary regulations, it is possible that the IRS or Tax Court will rule differently. My opinion is that it is not likely. Given the IRS' own promotion of Treas. Reg. § 1.25A-5, it is quite reasonable to assume that taxpayers can indeed "include [certain] scholarships in income to increase the education credit." If there is a change in procedure and processes for calculating qualifying expenses, I suspect that the IRS will provide additional guidance first.

Conservatism

Professional Conservatism is a valuable tool for protecting the liability of practitioners. While it is possible to make many arguments for their clients, it is often much safer to be conservative. In that case, consider how the IRS might rule is such situations and how the Tax Court might rule. If the taxpayer cannot irrefutably argue the case for a particular position, it may be wiser to assume the position that the IRS can make. Actual arguments with the IRS can be costly.

A review of the Internal Revenue Manual can be invaluable in understanding the standards that IRS agents follow in examining a return, and the types of information they may request from taxpayers. The manual can be accessed at www.irs.gov/irm. Searching the manual is not a native feature of the website, but most search engines support the site: option. To search a term in the manual, add *site:irs.gov/irm* to the search string.

Alternate Treatments

There are many preparers who do not take advantage of Treas. Reg. § 1.25A-5 to re-characterize scholarships, including them in income to increase the credit. The biggest reason is that they probably don't know about it. However, there are others who are aware of it but who do not fully take advantage of the regulations, possibly out of fear. Instead, they add other requirements that are not a part of the regulations.

One treatment is to limit the amount of qualifying expenses to "own money" or the amount paid out of pocket to the institution. This treatment has even been proposed or advised by some IRS personnel. A similar treatment is to limit the amount that can be re-characterized by the amount of non-qualifying expenses paid. One or both treatments could restrict the amounts to amounts paid through the institution. In both cases proponents read-into the regulations procedures that do not exist in the code or the text of the regulations.

The reasoning for these treatments lies in the way examples are worded in the regulations and the examples in Publication 970. When the example says an amount that is re-characterized as taxable "can" be used to pay non-qualifying expenses such as room and board, their assumption is that the amount "must" be used to pay non-qualifying expenses.

Another reason for these interpretations may be ignorance or misunderstanding of the forces of law. It's important to understand the difference between sources when considering tax positions. The following web site clearly describes the force of different types of information.

http://www.irs.gov/Tax-Professionals/Tax-Code,-Regulations-and-Official-Guidance

In summary, the Internal Revenue Code contains the law passed or amended by Congress and the regulations are provided by the IRS as a way to enforce the Internal Revenue Code. Together these two have the force of law. The Internal Revenue Code and Treasury Regulations are the sources cited in tax cases. There are other forms of documents, but the Internal Revenue Manual points out specifically that IRS publications do not have the force of law.

4.10.7.2.8 (01-01-2006)

IRS Publications

1. IRS Publications explain the law in plain language for taxpayers and their advisors. They typically highlight changes in the law, provide examples illustrating Service positions, and include worksheets. Publications are nonbinding on the Service and do not necessarily cover all positions for a given issue. While a good source of general information, publications should not be cited to sustain a position. [10]

Literal Interpretation

Following is an argument for the literal interpretation that I used in response to someone using one of the alternate treatment rules.

First, the regulations generally identify qualified expenses as amounts paid for a student, from any source.

Treas. Reg. 1.25A-5

(b) Educational expenses paid by a third party—

(1) In general. Solely for purposes of section 25A, if a third party (someone other than the taxpayer, the taxpayer's spouse if the taxpayer is treated as married within the meaning of section 7703, or a claimed dependent) makes a payment directly to an eligible educational institution to pay for a student's qualified tuition and related expenses, the student is treated as receiving the payment from the third party and, in turn, paying the qualified tuition and related expenses to the institution.

---

[10] http://www.irs.gov/irm/part4/irm_04-010-007.html

According to these regulations amounts paid for qualified expenses can be from any source, taxpayer, child, rich uncle, granny, and even scholarships and grants. No "own money" is required. That qualified expenses include amounts paid from scholarships and grants is further indicated by the next subsection

(c) Adjustment to qualified tuition and related expenses for certain excludable educational assistance—

(1) In general. In determining the amount of an education tax credit, qualified tuition and related expenses for any academic period must be reduced by the amount of any tax-free educational assistance allocable to such period. For this purpose, tax-free educational assistance means—

(i) A qualified scholarship that is excludable from income under section 117;

If scholarships and grants were not included in the amount of qualified expenses paid then you would not be able to reduce those expenses by that amount.

Note: The text makes it even clearer by saying **"the student is treated as receiving the payment from the third party and, in turn, paying the qualified tuition and related expenses to the institution."** There is no distinction based on the source. Everything is considered paid by the student.

Second, not only does the regulation define what qualified expenses are, it prescribes this as the method of adjusting them. Given the qualified expenses paid, the taxpayer reduces them by tax-free scholarship amounts. It's a very simple process.

Third, if the taxpayer can treat a scholarship amount (Pell grants) as taxable, he can choose NOT to reduce the expenses by that amount if he includes it in income.

(3) Scholarships and fellowship grants. For purposes of paragraph (c)(1)(i) of this section, a scholarship or fellowship grant is treated as a qualified scholarship excludable under section 117 except to the extent—

(i) The scholarship or fellowship grant (or any portion thereof) may be applied, by its terms, to expenses other than qualified tuition and related expenses within the meaning of section 117(b)(2) (such as room and board) and the student reports the grant (or the appropriate portion thereof) as income on the student's federal income tax return if the student is required to file a return; ...

That is also a simple process.

In one of my examples, the student had a Pell grant of $5,250 and qualifying expenses of $7,720 and reduced them by $3,720 tax-free scholarship money to get $4,000 in adjusted qualified expenses. The remaining scholarship funds ($5,250 - $3,720 = $1,530) are included in income. My method categorizes the expenses to make it understandable but returns the same results.

IRS Tips and notices summarize this very process in numerous places, including the 8863 instructions

> You may be able to increase the combined value of an education credit and certain educational assistance if the student includes some or all of the educational assistance in income in the year it is received.

That shows what to do (increase credit) and how to do it (include assistance in income).

Examples given in the publications and instructions are useful in giving scenarios, but they only illustrate the regulations. They don't alter them, and they certainly don't contradict them. All of the examples in the publications and instructions can be verified with the method given in Treasury Regulation 1.25A-5.

It's important to consider the tax code and IRS regulations, which are the definitive sources for tax law. Policies and procedures solely based on what can be surmised from IRS publications and examples do not constitute tax law. While the plain language of the regulations is unmistakable, the examples and other sources are indeed more obscure, but in my initial research of this subject I found few court decisions to clarify the regulations, probably because the law and regulations are so clear.

In summary, I don't think the IRS or Tax Court is going to say, "Okay you complied with requirements, but you did not fit into any of the examples given," and I don't think the examples can show any other intent that would change the simple procedures given in the regulations.

Conclusion

When clients mention educational expenses and then dismiss them because everything was covered by scholarships and other financial aid, ask to take a look and explain that they may be able to claim education credits of up to $2,500, especially if some of the expenses were paid with student loans or Pell grants.

Even better, use the annual tax questionnaire to let clients know of the potential credit, even if they do not receive a 1098T or are not out of pocket for any of the expenses. By understanding the regulations and the ability to treat scholarships as income, you can pleasantly surprise your clients. All that is needed is a little pre-season preparation, organization of client educational records, and a worksheet that calculates qualifying expenses used for the credit. Then see if that can be duplicated with prior year returns.

> *... Most Pell Grant recipients should claim at least $2,000 in tuition and fees for the AOTC, even if that means allocating some of their scholarship money to living expenses and counting those amounts as taxable income.*[11]
>
> *– Adam Looney, Deputy Assistant Secretary for Tax Analysis United States Department of the Treasury.*

---

[11] http://www.treasury.gov/connect/blog/Pages/Helping-students-and-families-access-college-tax-benefits.aspx

About the Author

Dana Bell has degrees in Accounting and Computer Information Systems. He graduated summa cum laude from the University of Texas at Tyler in 2012, and received his Enrolled Agent designation in 2014. He is also working toward CPA certification and hoping to land an accountant position at a local CPA firm.

In addition to writing about tax accounting and business, Dana is a computer programmer, website developer and host, database guru, and graphic designer (Adobe Certified Expert). Favorite pastimes include disc golf, photography, chess, and Scrabble™.

Professional and Social Media

LinkedIn: https://www.linkedin.com/in/dbell154/

Switched Keys (blog): http://www.tylerhosting.com/b2e/

Resume: http://www.tylerhosting.com/dbell/resume/

Personal Site: http://www.tylerhosting.com/dbell/

FaceBook: http://www.facebook.com/dbell154/

Twitter: http://www.twitter.com/dbell154/

LibraryThing: http://www.librarything.com/profile/dbell154/

Smashwords: https://www.smashwords.com/profile/view/dbell154/